Live Love Light and FRUITS

from
Olenko's Kitchen and Friends
Rainbow Diet Around The World

Aleksandra Winters

Olenko's Kitchen

For more information, please e-mail olenko@olenkoskitchen.com

The information in this book is not intended to diagnose or treat any disease and should not be construed as medical advice. Readers should seek their own professional counsel for any health or medical condition before embarking on a new or different way of eating.

First Edition Published in the United States of America 2017

www.OlenkosKitchen.com

Library of Congress Cataloging-in-Publication Data available upon request.

ISBN: 978-0-9971059-3-3

Live Love Light and Fruits from Olenko's Kitchen and Friends may be purchased for educational, business, or promotional use. For information on bulk purchases, please contact the sales department at sales@olenkoskitchen.com.

Some of the recipes and photographs have appeared in print or digital form.

All photography by Bill Winters and Aleksandra Winters

Book Cover Design by Daria Jabenko

Graphic Design by Heather Stalker, Crave Creative Group

Editing by Lidia Bis

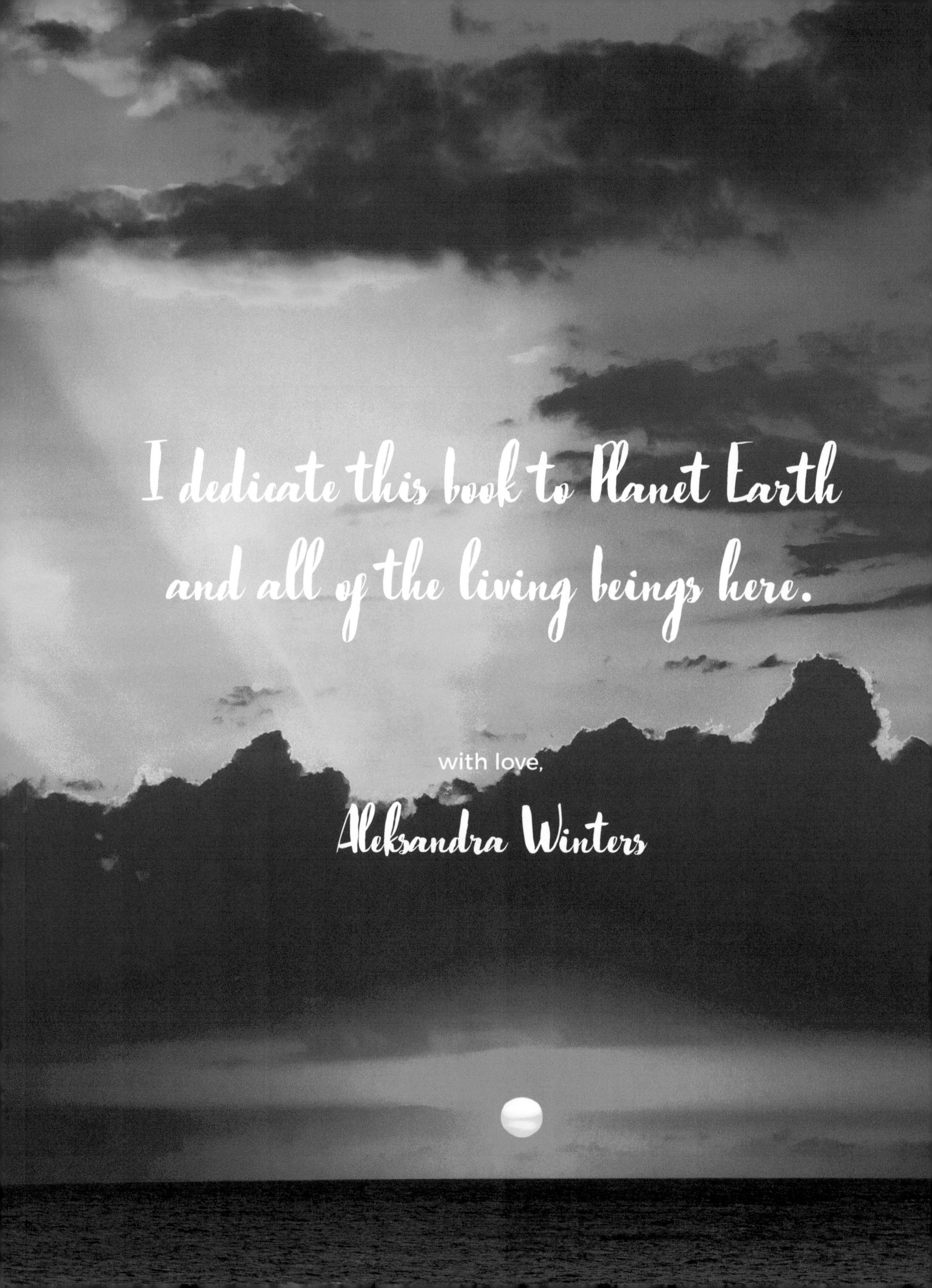

I dedicate this book to Planet Earth
and all of the living beings here.

with love,

Aleksandra Winters

Live your life to the fullest.

Love everything and everyone.

Light is in you, and

Eat *Fruits* and Veggies every day.

I am very grateful to all the amazing people who contributed recipes, including my family, friends, colleagues, students, and many others who have touched my soul and inspired me to create this book. You will find recipes from Poland, Italy, Morocco, Puerto Rico, Brazil, Thailand, South Korea, Peru, Norway, Russia, Australia, Israel, and many other countries—all inspired by flavors and spices from other cultures. I truly believe that life is about following your passion, sharing, caring, having joy, experimenting, learning, and collaborating. May you all be blessed with the abundance of nature's gifts.

table of contents

Chapter 9

FOOD IS MY LIFE.
WOULD YOU SHARE IT WITH ME?
I WILL MAKE YOU A SCRUMPTIOUS BREAKFAST 72

Chapter 10

LEAVE THE PAST IN THE PAST AND GO NUTS
FOR NUTTY AND CHEESY SIDE DISHES 85

Chapter 11

WHAT'S SO SPICY ABOUT SPICES AND FRESH ABOUT HERBS?   102

Chapter 12

IT'S LUNCHTIME: SALAD OR SOUP A DAY KEEPS THE DOCTOR AWAY!   109

Chapter 13

LIFE IS SHORT. EAT DESSERT FIRST. SWEETS THAT ARE SO YUMMY THAT THEY WILL MAKE YOU SING IN YOUR TUMMY! **126**

Chapter 14

PEAS TO THE WORLD WITH HAPPY VEGGIES FOR DINNER   157

Chapter 15

NATURE'S GIFTS FROM THE BAR   182

CHAPTER 1

The Rocking Rainbow Diet

If you want to be strong
And have energy to live and play,
Eat veggies and fruits every day!

You cannot deny
That a variety of rainbow diet
Will make your day shine!

Oranges are sour and sweet,
And they have a lot of antioxidants and vitamin C,
But spice them up with cayenne in the smoothie
To make them more groovy.

Blueberry pancakes are yummy with blueberry
smoothie,
But treat them with happiness and kindness
To turn them into a spectacular goody.

Ordinary chocolate pancakes aren't that healthy,
But supercharge them with raw cacao and walnuts
To make them extra wealthy.

Bananas like to change
Every now and then.
First they are green, then they are yellow,
Till it comes to an end
And they become spotty, mushy, and mellow.

Try to love all your greens
And make them dance
In your smoothie and juice machines!

I am not going to lie
That I really love basil, parsley, mint, and chives.
I mix greens like cilantro, spinach, Swiss chard, and
kale with lemon,
Then add cucumbers and a watermelon!

And remember, corn is corny, but it's good for you,
And you can add it to salads and make a healthy
corn stew!

Carrots are yummy,
And they will sing beautifully
With broccoli in your tummy!

Veggies are good,
I will not lie,
But I still love a sweet cherry pie!

Chipmunks go nuts for nuts,
Cows like a wheatgrass smoothie
When pigs fly high
And eat a key-lime pie!

Raw peanut butter cups are guilt-free,
Yummy, and sweet.
They will make you feel gorgeous,
Look healthy, and fit.

If you drink coffee, juice, water, and wine,
That's fine,
Just make them intertwine!

And don't give me baloney;
I know you love pasta and macaroni!
Instead, use your Spirooli
To make healthy veggie macaroni!

Rainbow food can be chewy.
It can be
Crunchy,
Sweet, Salty,
Colorful, and Dewy.

So remember, use all the colors of the rainbow.
Dance the cha-cha with beans
And tango with mango!
Find your inner truth
And dance your own fruity moves.

Throw the stressful life away.
Do yoga, meditate, and
Eat your fruits and veggies
every day.
Bless nature.
Have some water, chill, and pray.

Working on your own happiness first
Is not selfish
Or self-obsessed.

So enjoy your health
And create spiritual wealth!

Find your joy! Love!
Sparkle more,
Forgive, forget, move on,
And rejoice.

Follow your happiness
And passion,
And live your life with
Kindness and compassion.

When you live your life this way,
You benefit yourself
And inspire
Others as well.

Hi

My mother told me not to play with my food, but I do.

Hello, Gorgeous! I'm so happy you are joining me on a culinary journey around the world. I'm Aleksandra, a.k.a. Olenko in Polish. I am an intuitive chef, a health and wellness coach, an artist, an art educator, and the author of ***Raw Food Art: Four Seasons of Plant-Powered Goodness*** cookbook. I have been working for over fifteen years with thousands of people on transitioning their relationship with food. The process begins when we choose to create a loving relationship with our body and align our mind to make the healthiest food choices. On this journey, we find the path to wellness, great health, spirituality, and inner peace.

I was born and raised behind the iron curtain in communist Poland – a drab pessimistic environment devoid of color, consisting mostly of blacks, grays, and whites. This lack of color and vibrancy in my life motivated me to seek out a bold way to express myself in a colorful way.

My love for the colors of the rainbow started at the age of five - the first time I cooked in the kitchen with my grandmother. I can remember it vividly! It was a beautiful, sunny day outside, and my grandmother said she would show me how to make authentic Polish pierogis. I remember wandering through the garden with her as she showed me how to pick the most perfect vegetables for our meal.

I watched closely and listened to my grandmother's wise words. I knew there was something special happening in our garden - never in my life had I been surrounded by such color, vibrancy, and life! Years later, I looked back and realized that this simple moment in the garden and cooking my first meal was when I discovered my passion for cooking and the arts! As a family, we continued to create the most delicious, healthy, and colorful meals for years to come. Even to this day, I am proud to say that my family still maintains their huge, organic garden at their home.

My love for cooking had a humble beginning, but the passion behind it has developed immensely over the years. I founded Olenko's Kitchen to share my enthusiasm and expertise with people and to help them reach their optimal health. I received a Plant-Based Nutrition Certification from Dr. T. Campbell at Cornell University. I am also a certified Integrative Nutrition Health and Lifestyle Coach by the Institute for Integrative Nutrition. I provide group and private coaching via Skype or telephone for my clients around the world. I teach in person and online cooking classes. I decided to write this book to address questions that my clients and friends so often ask me. You can find more information about my programs at www.OlenkosKitchen.com

I currently reside in the New York City Metropolitan area. I have been living here since 1998. I love New York City! The most exciting thing about New York is that it is always changing. It is a marvelous place to be; there are people from all over the world, and there are many restaurants (even Polish ones!), museums, and lots of places to see! Life in New York plays a big role in my cooking. With more than 800 languages spoken in the city, New York is a hub for many ethnic stores and restaurants where you can find flavors from every corner of the world. Just imagine how many variations of ethnic food you can find! I continue to learn about new cultures and new cuisines, and I happily meet amazing friends along the way! Because New York City is such an international location, my friends are from all over the world! What is extra special about this book is that the recipes inside are from myself and the most talented people I know - my friends!

I live in a spectacular city, although throughout my life, I have been fortunate enough to travel the world! My food is very much influenced by many wonders of the world and my worldwide explorations. I have met people of all cultures and, with every person I met, I took a bit of their culture with me. What can I say? My bliss comes from learning and adventure! I have watched beautiful sunsets in Hawaii, walked the crowded streets of Tokyo, and climbed the Great Wall of China. I have meditated inside the Great Pyramid of Giza, picked fragrant spices in the streets of Marrakesh, and discovered ancient Mayan temples in Mexico. I have visited raw cacao and coffee plantations in Jamaica, tasted exotic durian in Thailand, and participated in a traditional Bedouin barbecue in Petra. I take cooking classes and learn from locals every place I visit.

The adventure doesn't stop there! Each of my recipes is inspired by shapes and colors of nature. Nature is my muse. It inspires me to create my art and unconventional, eclectic recipes. Nature grounds me, balances me, and brings me inner peace. Although I love the busy life in New York City, I always find peace and my center when I reconnect with nature. Nature is the answer to everything. This is the advice I always give to my clients and friends: eat more natural foods; spend more time in nature to find joy, happiness, and balance; get fresh air and more sun; and move your body.

In addition, in this book you will find many tips for how to create a healthy and happy life. When you live from a place of inner peace, joy, love, kindness, and compassion, you will intuitively choose the right foods for your body at any particular moment. You deserve to have a glorious life and an energetic, thriving, and beautiful body. Follow your passion. Be happy. Be you. Keep shining your beautiful light. Trust your body. Trust life. Follow your intuition. Be in sync with nature and the course of life. Rejoice in every moment. Fill your heart with gratitude. Take control of your life. Shake up your beliefs. Shake up your pantry and your kitchen.

Setting the mood in your kitchen is very important. Opt for dynamic flavors, shapes, and colors. Surround your house and kitchen with beautiful, colorful, and organic fruits and veggies.

I could not be more grateful that you are here to explore an international array of foods with me. My wish is that this book will encourage you to create a healthy lifestyle and empower you into action by incorporating simple, natural foods into your diet. Let the rainbow diet inspire you. Let each delicious bite take you on a journey around the world. Live freely and have fun! With Olenko's Kitchen, you will find joy in cooking your own food, be harmonious with nature, and see all the colors of the rainbow around you! Enjoy!

Here's to life!
Here's to joy!
Here's to happy
food!

Let's raise our
glasses to happy
rainbow foods!

No restrictions, no
rules! Eat the diet
you want!

Food is love.
Food is medicine.
Food is energy.
Food has vibration.

CHAPTER 2

Olenko's Kitchen Revolution

My mother told me I made a revolution in the kitchen, and now you can too!

Spread love! Live your life with joy! Be you! Break the rules! Make a revolution in your kitchen! Have fun! Dance the abundance dance with fruits and veggies! This is what Olenko's Kitchen is all about!

EAT THE RAINBOW EVERY DAY

Plants have amazing properties. They can communicate with one another. They can heal us and restore our mind, body, and spirit. Plants are very powerful. There are tremendous health benefits of a rainbow diet, but you may wonder what a rainbow diet is.

When you consume a fresh and colorful variety of whole, organic, plant-based foods daily, you are eating a rainbow diet. Simple as that! Our ancestors knew that eating a vast spectrum of colorful fresh produce would fill them with energy, lift their mood, and help them thrive. Every color found in natural food—such as green, blue, red, yellow, orange, purple, and white—has a unique nutritional value. The more diverse your diet is, the better you will feel.

Find joy, longevity, vitality, and happiness when you choose rainbow diet foods. Incorporate fresh, organic fruits, greens, nuts, seeds, healthy grains, and vegetables into your everyday food recipes. When you fuel your body with amazing foods, you will feel fabulous.

I don't follow any rules in the kitchen. I am an intuitive chef and artist, so I feel my way around food. I don't usually measure ingredients, and I experiment with unusual flavors to achieve an unusual taste. I eat pizza and ice cream for breakfast, and brownies and chocolate for dessert. I don't skip meals. I don't starve myself. I don't cut carbs. I snack between meals. I am a chocolate queen.

I do all these things, and I am happy, healthy, and full of energy. How do I do it? It's very simple: I follow my intuition and use natural, whole, plant-based ingredients to make out-of-this-world dishes. I create a revolution in the kitchen, although my mother always told me not to.

I have two helpers in my kitchen: my cats Kizia Mizia and Sushi. In addition to cat food, Kizia Mizia loves her greens. A day cannot pass by without her having some spinach, cucumbers, or seaweed. Unlike his sister, Sushi doesn't eat greens, but he loves to play with fruits and veggies. His favorite snacks are fresh catnip and peppermint.

Many recipes in this book can be mixed and matched. You can take sauce or cheese from one recipe and use it with another. For example, make a smoothie and serve it over rice, quinoa, veggie pasta, or steel oats. This way, possibilities are endless, and you will have fun experimenting in the kitchen. Let your imagination run wild.

COMMON QUESTIONS

To help you consider the transition to this healthy and essential way of living, let's discuss some of the questions I so often hear about the rainbow diet.

Why should I consider switching to a plant-based diet?

- You are sick and need to change your lifestyle.
- You feel tired all the time.
- You drink a lot of coffee to sustain you throughout the day.
- You do not like the way you look.
- You have experienced a significant life event and feel the urge to reinvent yourself.
- You know that a change would serve you well, and you are ready to embrace it.

Regardless of the reason for change, it must come from within. Evaluate your life, and analyze how the food you choose makes you feel.

Eating plants will make a huge difference to your health. Too much fat and animal protein can clog our arteries and lead to heart problems, diabetes, cancer, and obesity. Research proves that a plant-based/vegan/vegetarian diet can help prevent those diseases and even reverse some existing conditions. Dr. T. Colin Campbell, a biochemist who specializes in the effect of nutrition on long-term health and the author of The China Study, states,

the SAD diet—consists of soda, fatty snacks, salt, processed sugar, artificial ingredients, preservatives, and additives. We don't exercise. We spend long hours in front of computers or TVs, which leads to obesity and other health issues. We all need to eat more plants daily. Dr. Caldwell Esselstyn, a physician and the author of Prevent and Reverse Heart Disease, claims, "Some people think plant-based diet, whole foods diet is extreme. Half a million people a year will have their chests opened up and a vein taken from their leg and sewn onto their coronary artery. Some people would call that extreme."

I have followed a plant-based diet for many years and am a living example of its benefits. Some people think a vegan/plant-based diet is about restrictions. They don't realize that vegans consume a variety of amazing foods daily. This diet is excellent for our health and provides minerals, vitamins, protein, fiber, energy, life force, enzymes, and phytonutrients. The best part is that these foods are very flavorful and can be guilt-free.

WHAT ARE THE DIFFERENCES BETWEEN A RAW FOOD DIET, A VEGETARIAN DIET, A VEGAN DIET, A PLANT-BASED DIET, AND A RAINBOW DIET?

"Today, more than ninety-five percent of all chronic disease is caused by food choice, toxic food ingredients, nutritional deficiencies, and lack of physical exercise."

— *Mike Adams, the Health Ranger*

"I know of nothing else in medicine that can come close to what a plant-based diet can do. In theory, if everyone were to adopt this, I really believe we can cut health care costs by seventy to eighty percent. That's amazing. And it all comes from understanding nutrition, applying nutrition, and just watching the results."

Unfortunately, most people don't eat enough fresh fruits and vegetables. The standard American diet—

Vegan Diet

Vegans don't use any animal products for food, fashion, or beauty (cosmetics). They don't consume dairy, eggs, honey, meat, or fish. Many vegans choose this lifestyle for ethical reasons. If you love animals and want to help them, go vegan!

Animal agriculture has a tremendous impact on world hunger. Consuming meat is one of the most harmful things people do to Planet Earth. Industrial farming is very wasteful and inefficient compared to growing plants to feed people. Large amounts of crops must be grown to support the raising of factory farm animals.

We feed and slaughter 60 billion farm animals every year, and there are only 7.3 billion humans on earth. Think about that. Factory farming is the biggest human-caused source of greenhouse gases and land use. It also causes water pollution, rainforest destruction, and land degradation.

Raw Vegan Diet

A raw vegan diet allows you to eat fruits, vegetables, nuts, and seeds in their raw state, which preserves the most nutrients and enzymes. Any kind of food prepared below 118°F is considered raw. My first book, ***Raw Food Art: Four Seasons of Plant-Powered Goodness,*** is all about raw vegan food and its benefits.

People on a raw food diet consume a lot of smoothies, juices, salads, soups, and veggie pastas. Some people make gourmet raw food by dehydrating ingredients to create pizza, crackers, bread, brownies, cookies, and so on.

Vegetarian Diet

Those on a vegetarian diet eat plant-based food, but many include dairy, eggs, and honey in their diets. Vegetarians do not consume fish or meat.

Pescatarian Diet

A pescatarian diet promotes eating plant-based food along with fish, seafood, dairy, eggs, and honey. Pescatarians do not consume meat.

Whole Plant-Based Diet

A whole plant-based diet promotes the eating of natural foods like fruits, vegetables, whole grains, seeds, nuts, and honey. People who follow this diet avoid processed food and drinks, fast food, and unhealthy oils. This diet promotes food that is as close to its natural state as possible—just as nature intended. The more natural the food we eat, the better.

People who follow a whole plant-based diet are less likely to develop cancer, diabetes, or high blood pressure. Much research has been conducted to prove the benefits of a whole plant-based diet. Dr. T. Colin Campbell further stated, "The ideal human diet looks like this: Consume plant-based foods in forms as close to their natural state as possible ("whole" foods). Eat a variety of vegetables, fruits, raw nuts and seeds, beans and legumes, and whole grains. Avoid heavily processed foods and animal products. Stay away from added salt, oil, and sugar. Aim to get eighty percent of your calories from carbohydrates, ten percent from fat, and ten percent from protein." For more information, refer to studies by Dr. T. Colin Campbell, Dr. Thomas M. Campbell, Dr. John A. McDougall, Dr. Caldwell Esselstyn, Dr. Michael Greger, Dr. Neal Barnard, Dr. Michael A. Klaper, Dr. Dean Ornish, Dr. Joel Fuhrman, and many others.

Olenko's Kitchen Rainbow Diet

My diet advocates incorporating all of nature's colors into your meals. The food on your plate should be as colorful as a rainbow to provide a wide range of necessary nutrients to your body. Fruits and vegetables are chock-full of antioxidants and phytochemicals that fight and ward off diseases. The rainbow diet has no restrictions.

To follow the rainbow diet, eat more raw foods whenever possible. Go vegan or switch to plant-based meals even a few times a week. A raw, vegan, whole-food, plant-based diet is rich in fiber and very beneficial to our health.

Not all vegan diets are healthy. Someone on a plant-based diet could be eating lots of junk food—such as potato chips, candy, or French fries—and drinking sugary sodas. And vice versa: many meat eaters can be healthy if they pay attention to their choices and include fruits and vegetables. The goal is to eat as much natural food as you can and avoid preservatives, artificial ingredients, and GMOs (genetically modified organisms).

Your lifestyle choices have a tremendous impact on the earth. The United Nations has called for a global shift to a vegan/plant-based diet. The report from United Nations Environment Programme's (UNEP) international panel of sustainable resource management states, "As the global population surges towards a predicted 9.1 billion people by 2050, western tastes for diets rich in meat and dairy products are unsustainable. Impacts from agriculture are expected to increase substantially due to population growth increasing consumption of animal products. Unlike fossil fuels, it is difficult to look for alternatives: people have to eat. A substantial reduction of impacts would only be possible with a substantial worldwide diet change, away from animal products." According to professor Edgar Hertwich, the lead author of the report, "Animal products cause more damage than [producing] construction minerals, such as sand or cement, plastics, or metals. Biomass and crops for animals are as damaging as [burning] fossil fuels." Your eating choices will help prevent climate change, world hunger, and ecological devastation, besides impacting your own health and the lives of many animals. We only have one home: Planet Earth. If we keep polluting and destroying our home, where will we live?

Choose locally grown food as much as possible, support sustainable businesses, and eat more plants every day. Eat the rainbow every day!

You and the Environment

We all share one Mother Earth, so don't be wasteful. I was taught to not waste anything, including food, water, electricity, or money. When I was growing up in a communist Poland, we had to be very frugal and resourceful. Even now, when I live in the United States, one of the richest countries in the world, I make sure to turn off the light when I leave the room, turn off the water when I brush my teeth, use leftover food, reuse biodegradable bags and containers, recycle, avoid using plastic, and much more.

> "You don't have to cook fancy or complicated masterpieces – just good food from fresh ingredients."
>
> – Julia Child

I am very mindful of the imprint I leave on the environment. Many people do not realize how much food and energy they waste every day. We all share one Mother Earth, so we should not pollute it or abuse it.

How Do I Decide Which Diet Is Best For Me?

Today, when technology and social media dominate our lives, there is so much contradictory information. We're overwhelmed by the number of people claiming to be gurus, specialists, and coaches. We're confused about diets and their benefits. As a result, it's hard for people to decide which approach is right for them.

Sometimes it's best to disregard other people's opinions. Focus on what your body is telling you. You may even have to disregard what you previously learned from your family, friends, or your own culture, and go within to connect with your inner self. Listen to what your body is trying to communicate. Your body is such an amazing phenomenon. It will tell you which foods to choose and which to avoid. Have you watched animals forage for food? They instinctively choose what their body needs at that moment. You can, too.

If you're new to having a meaningful relationship with your food, starting a journal may be helpful. Take note of how much you eat in a day, what cravings you have, and how you feel after eating a particular food. But don't get too stressed about it. Have fun with your food experimentation: try an exotic fruit you've never had and choose a colorful variety of fresh produce every day.

I Have Tried Many Diets but Failed Every Time. How Can I Make this Work?

Don't make your diet too strict or rigid. If you deprive yourself of what your body asks for, sooner or later, you will bounce back and binge on your craved food. If you've been following a SAD diet, you probably won't transition to super-healthy habits right away. The process varies from person to person and may take time. The transition is contingent on many factors, such as how long you've been eating an unhealthy diet, how much junk food you've been eating, your family cooking tradition, your culture's cooking customs, your health and motivation, your willingness to change your eating habits, your determination, your attitude and outlook on life, and so on.

You may think you eat healthfully, but instead, you've been eating the wrong kinds of food. The raw food diet, for example, is full of nuts. It is high in fat. If you eat that kind of food often, you'll not meet your dietary expectations.

It takes sixteen to twenty tries for our taste buds to adapt to a new flavor. If you've been eating junk food full of processed sugar and artificial ingredients most of your life, your taste buds will not jump for joy the first time you try beets or kale. Be persistent; don't give up.

The food you choose and the effect it has on you may depend on your body type, the job you do, your overall health, the climate you live in, and more. Eskimos, for example, need a hearty diet to counterbalance the harsh conditions they live in, but their lifespan is, on average, significantly shorter than that of people in warmer climates. There is no perfect diet and no magical fix or pill that will make you shed weight instantly. Find your own style and feel what works for you and what does not.

> "It's never too late to start eating well. A good diet can reverse many health conditions. In short: change the way you eat and you can transform your health for the better."
>
> – Dr. T. Colin Campbell

What Do You Eat In a Day?

My clients always ask me this question. They think I am hungry all the time. The truth is that I eat so much nutritional food that I don't feel restricted or deprived at all. Come to my house, and you will see the abundance of fruits and vegetables that I surround myself with. I always have plenty of food, and I love to share it with my neighbors, friends, coworkers, and family.

The food I eat depends mostly on what is available in season. I try to eat seasonal, local, and organic foods as much as possible. My typical menu for the day looks like this:

- I start with a glass of room-temperature water with half a lemon.
- For breakfast, I make a smoothie to bring to work. If I am home, I will make vegetable juice, a fruit salad, chia porridge, or overnight oats. Occasionally on the weekends, I will make healthy pancakes or waffles. Sometimes I have coffee or Teeccino with spices and nut milk or herbal tea.
- For lunch, I usually have a huge salad. I love salads of any kind. I always bring a rainbow salad and fruit to work, such as an orange or an apple. Sometimes I have a garlic-avocado sandwich or soup.
- For an afternoon snack, I love to have hot tea with raw chocolate, a truffle, a cookie, or more fruit. I love fruit!
- For dinner, I have a vegetable soup with beans, tofu, or noodles; a stew with quinoa or sweet potatoes; and another salad garnished with parsley, cilantro, mint, or basil (as you can see, I really love salads!). Sometimes I have healthy cooked pasta, raw zucchini pasta, vegan sushi, or a rainbow pizza. I make a different dinner every day, and I love to keep my menu interesting.
- In the evening, I may have fruit, fresh juice, raw coconut milk, or golden turmeric milk.
- Throughout the day, I drink lots of water to stay hydrated.

My diet consists of seventy to eighty percent raw food—even more in the summer. In the winter, I may eat more cooked or steamed foods, but I always eat tons of fresh fruits, veggies, and salads, and I drink fresh juice. My favorite fruits are bananas, watermelons, cherries, and persimmons. It is important to eat the rainbow every day so that we get the whole spectrum of vitamins, minerals, and fiber. My food on the plate is always simple, healthy, colorful, tasty, and made with love. It is certainly never boring!

Try this kind of diet for yourself for twenty-one days and see how it makes you feel. If you are interested in learning more about raw food, check out my first cookbook, *Raw Food Art: Four Seasons of Plant-Powered Goodness*.

I Only Shop at Health Food Stores, So I'm Okay, Right?

Not necessarily. Just because something comes from a health food store does not mean that it is healthy. If you buy packaged food, chances are it contains many ingredients, including preservatives. Some of the ingredients may be harmful to your body. It is always better to buy whole ingredients and make the food by yourself.

Food and soil are not the way they used to be when your grandparents were children. Food used to be better; it used to be real. GMOs were unheard of, soil was not depleted of its nutrients, and there was no excess of packaged, processed, and fast food. It is up to you to regain control of your life and your food.

Read the labels, educate yourself, listen to your body, follow your intuition, and learn to recognize how the food you eat makes you feel. If the product contains more than five to eight ingredients, choose another one with fewer ingredients that you can actually understand. Use the following quotation by Michael Pollan as your guidance: "If it came from a plant, eat it; if it was made in a plant, don't."

I Would Like to Eat Healthy, But I Don't Have Time to Cook.

It always surprises me when clients and friends tell me they don't have time to cook. To me, it's like saying that you want to live a healthy life but don't have time to breathe. You wouldn't put cheap gas in an expensive car, would you? These days, we do all sorts of unhealthy things and expect miracles. Our bad habits, such as inactivity and wrong food choices, put our health in jeopardy. Yet health is our greatest wealth. Don't say that you don't have time to cook. Make the time.

Tip Sheet

QUICK, HEALTHY MEALS AT HOME

There are twenty-four hours in a day for everyone. You only have one life, so nourish yourself. You may be healthy at the moment, but when you get older, you may wish you had taken better care of yourself. Let food be thy medicine and medicine be thy food.

YOUR FREEZER IS YOUR FRIEND. Cook in large quantities and save leftovers for the next day. Or, freeze extra portions for a time when you come home tired and hungry. Keep frozen vegetables (corn, peas, string beans, etc.) and fruits (blueberries, strawberries, cherries, peaches, mango, etc.) in the freezer to make a quick dinner or snack. I like to have frozen pesto and add it to cooked pasta. This way, dinner can be ready within ten minutes.

A WELL-STOCKED PANTRY. Stock your pantry with brown rice, healthy pasta, quinoa, jars of tomato sauce, canned coconut milk, olives, and sun-dried tomatoes to make fast dishes. Choose healthy ingredients that are quick-cooking, such as quinoa, rice pasta, or lentils. Soak beans overnight or before you leave for work. When you come home, they will be ready to cook and will be done very fast.

PLAN YOUR MEALS AHEAD OF TIME. You will make dinner faster if you don't waste time by looking at what is in your fridge and trying to decide what to make. Plan and prep your meals ahead of time. Chop veggies the night before. Make juice the night before and bring it to work. Soak almonds overnight. You can make nut milk when you get up. Make overnight oats. Your breakfast will be ready by the time you get up. Prep a salad before you go to bed. Take it with you to work.

DON'T FORGET DESSERT. When you make healthy desserts—such as popsicles, raw chocolate, brownies, or cookies—freeze some in a glass container and enjoy as a healthy treat any time. Always keep a healthy sweet on hand for those cravings!

I Would Like to Eat More Organic Produce, But It Is So Expensive.

While shopping for food, remember that your mighty dollar has more power than you think. By buying the products that you like, you create a greater demand for them; you vote for the products. Therefore, choose healthy, local, and organic options. Let the manufacturers of processed food know that you will not spend your hard-earned money on something that is not good for you.

"Going green doesn't start with doing green acts—it starts with a shift in consciousness. This shift allows you to recognize that with every choice you make, you are voting either for or against the kind of world you wish to see. When you assume this as a way of being, your choices become easier."

– Ian Somerhalder

Have you heard the saying, "If your grandma would not recognize it as food, don't buy it"? Most of the food today has been processed so much that it is far away from its natural form. If you pay attention to the ingredients, you will notice that most of them are chemical additives, preservatives, emulsifiers, and artificial colorings that you don't want to ingest. The shorter the list of the ingredients, the better.

You also want to avoid GMO ingredients, which are omnipresent in processed food. This is a major reason why buying organic is a much smarter choice, since you are investing in your own health. Would you rather buy cheap food now and spend thousands of dollars on medical bills later? Organic food is clean and helps your body heal itself.

Conventional fruit and vegetables are heavily sprayed with pesticides and herbicides, which are very powerful and toxic chemicals. Organic farming does not use pesticides but natural ways of fertilizing and repelling pests. If more people started buying organic, it would become more affordable. Therefore, as a society, we should demand more healthy food and less junk food, because what you put in your mouth is one of the most important decisions that you make every day.

Don't I Need Meat to Get My Protein?

No, you don't. Plants contain protein. As a matter of fact, plants contain all the vitamins and nutrients that your body needs to be healthy. Think about the largest animals, such as elephants, giraffes, and gorillas. They only consume plants, and yet they have big muscles. While we eat a plant-based diet, we can thrive because it is easy for the body to transform the food into energy without straining our digestive system.

Meat, on the other hand, takes very long to digest. It can cause inflammation, cancer, diabetes, heart disease, and more. That is why it is important to "eat the rainbow" to ensure that you are getting all the nutrients you need.

What Are Superfoods?

You have probably heard the word superfoods and wondered what those are. A superfood is a nutrient-rich food considered to be especially beneficial for health and well-being. In my opinion, all plant-based foods are superfoods because they all have unique superpowers. Very often, the term superfood is used by specific companies promoting a product, while the food itself may not be recognized by scientists as a superfood.

The following information can help you make the most of superfoods:

• Superfoods like moringa and spirulina can be used in smoothies, juices, and tonics.

• Fruits like pomegranates, dates, and wild blueberries can be mixed with your regular food.

• Green superfoods like kale, spinach, or dandelion can be consumed raw to ensure nutrition density.

• Chia or hemp seeds can be added to cereals, smoothies, and soups to add texture.

• Seaweed—such as dulse, kelp, or nori—can be added to salads or soups.

• Chaga or reishi mushroom powders can be added to raw chocolates, smoothies, or healthy elixirs.

Ask about superfoods next time you visit a health food store. You will be surprised to see a wide variety. They come as seeds, nuts, and powders; can be freeze-dried or fresh; and are even in capsules, so there is no excuse to not incorporate them in your diet.

What Vegetables Should I Eat?

Vegetables are gluten-free, fat-free, nutrient-packed superfoods. Include plenty of vegetables in your diet.

Healthy choices include the following, and many more:

- alfalfa sprouts
- asparagus
- broccoli
- cabbage
- celery
- collards
- garlic
- green beans
- kale
- lettuce
- onions
- radishes
- scallions
- spinach
- water chestnuts
- artichokes
- bok choy
- Brussels sprouts
- cauliflower
- chard
- fennel
- ginger
- jicama
- leek
- mushrooms
- parsley
- sauerkraut
- shallots
- turnip
- watercress

How Can I Incorporate Healthy Substitutes Into Traditional Cooking?

If you cook in a traditional way—and that tradition involves plenty of oil, salt, and heavy cream—here are some tips for healthier substitutes:

Salt. Use Himalayan, Celtic, or sea salt instead of table salt. Table salt has been processed so extensively that it has been stripped of its natural minerals, whereas Himalayan salt contains over eighty naturally occurring minerals necessary to your body. In order to preserve those minerals, make sure that you do not add Himalayan salt to the food while it is still cooking, but rather add at the very end, after you have turned off the heat, or when the food is on your plate.

Oil. Most oils become carcinogenic when heated to high temperatures. As with salt, add a little bit of coconut oil at the very end of cooking, after you have

lettuce

mush

Brussel Sprouts

asparagus

water chestnuts

CHARD

Collards

parsley

ginger

green beans

watercress

kale

ooms

alfalfa sprouts

ARTICHOKES

onions & shallots

celery

broccoli

Fennel

Spinach

bok choy

turnips

cabbage

RADISHES

jicama

turned off the heat. Opt for coconut oil, as it has many beneficial properties. I cook mostly oil-free, but if I do cook with oil, I choose coconut oil, which I add to my plate.

Avoid canola, safflower, and sunflower oils, even the organic ones, as they have been heavily processed, are GMO, and can be harmful to your body. You can simply use a dash of water on a skillet if you want to warm up leftovers from the day before, and add a little bit of oil at the end.

Healthy Fats. It is always better to use fat contained in whole produce instead of extracted oil. Sources of healthy fat include avocados, coconuts, olives, nuts and nut butters, vegan nut cheese, and seeds (flax seeds, sunflower seeds, pumpkin seeds, hemp seeds, sesame seeds, and chia seeds). Be conscious, however, of the high fat content foods you choose. Depending on your health goal, it may be better to choose baked or cooked foods instead of raw. For example, a baked cake may not be as heavy as a raw nut cake. Nuts and seeds are more fattening than flour. If you are trying to lose weight, avoid creamy sauces and dressings, cook oil-free, eat a lot of salads, and cut down on heavy items.

Cream. If you want to transition toward plant-based ingredients, replace dairy cream with nut cream or nut milk, such as cashew, almond, coconut, etc. These are very simple and quick to make. All you need are nuts and water.
For cashew milk, you do not have to soak the cashews, as they are the softest nuts. Simply blend cashews with water in a high-speed blender until you reach a smooth consistency. Add cashew cream to your plate as you would salt and oil, not to the pot while the food is still cooking. Store the rest in a glass jar in the refrigerator. It will stay fresh for a few days. You can do the same with other nuts, such as almonds or macadamia nuts, but they will have to be soaked first.

Sugar. Processed sugar contributes to many degenerative diseases, such as cancer and diabetes. There are many healthier options to choose from when you need to sweeten your dessert, coffee, tea, or favorite beverage. Try using dates, maple syrup, yacon syrup, SUGAR 2.0, coconut nectar, coconut sugar, or monk-fruit sweetener.

How Do I Bake With Gluten-Free Flour?
When it comes to baking, every time you use an alternative ingredient, expect a different end result. Gluten acts like a glue, so when you use flour with gluten, it binds ingredients together and makes the dough stretchable. Gluten-free flours are made from grains and seeds and do not glue ingredients together. If you use wrong proportions of gluten-free flour in baking, the dough may be very dense and will not rise. It will resemble a cardboard. You can use gluten-free flour in some recipes, but not all, so experiment with the proportions and texture first.

When you substitute one kind of flour with another, expect different results in texture, taste, and appearance. There are a wide variety of different kinds of flour to choose from. The following are gluten-free flours: bean, banana, green pea, amaranth, corn, cornstarch, cornmeal, millet, oat, rice, sorghum, teff, buckwheat, wild rice, almond, chestnut, coconut, flaxseed meal, hemp, mesquite, quinoa, chia seeds (salba), potato, potato starch, arrowroot, acorn, and tapioca. All these are naturally gluten-free. However, if they have been processed in a plant that also handles wheat, they may be contaminated with gluten. Therefore, in order to guarantee that the flour is gluten-free, look for a gluten-free claim on the package.

Most of these flours are nutrition-dense and rich in protein, calcium, iron, fiber, folate, thiamin, niacin, B-6, magnesium, phosphorus, potassium, and more. When you use them in baking, you will usually combine your gluten-free flour with other flour, not exceeding twenty-five percent of any flour blend in your recipe. Some gluten-free flours are available in dark and light varieties and are fine-, medium-, or coarse-milled. Select the right flour for your baking needs. You may not want to choose dark flour for delicate recipes.

To Starch or Not to Starch?
Many people think that carbohydrates are unhealthy and fattening, and they starve themselves to avoid it. In fact, there are many kinds of starches that will give you sustainable energy, keep you full for hours, or even help you lose weight. Healthy sources of starch include whole grains and seeds, such as quinoa (red, white, and black), rice (brown, wild, forbidden, jasmine, etc), barley, bulgur, teff, amaranth, and oats.

You can also get starch from root vegetables, such as sweet and purple potatoes, white potatoes, parsnips, rutabagas, and any form of winter squash, such as acorn, pumpkin, butternut, or spaghetti. Of course, it all depends on how you prepare them. If you cook, steam, or bake them, they are great and very nutritious, but if you eat French fries and potato chips, they will not be so healthy, unless you use an oil-free air fryer.

Pasta.

Another good source of starch is pasta, which is fast and easy to make. These days, there are many kinds of pasta and noodles that will help you create healthy, low-fat dishes. Pasta made from wheat and related grains in the wheat family—such as barley, rye, spelt, farro, and bulgur—contain gluten.

Most people enjoy products that contain gluten without any side effects. However, there are people who are allergic or sensitive to gluten. These individuals may choose gluten-free pasta, such as bean, quinoa, or buckwheat pasta; seaweed noodles; and raw noodles made with zucchini, squash, carrots, cucumbers, beets, yams, or sweet potatoes. For the raw pasta, use a Spirooli tool.

You can cook, steam, or bake your veggie pasta. These pastas are excellent to try with a variety of sauces. The choices can satisfy even the pickiest eater. My favorite pasta is quinoa-corn. For more ideas, look in my first cookbook, **_Raw Food Art: Four Seasons of Plant-Powered Goodness._**

If you can tolerate gluten, you can enjoy regular pasta. There are many wheat pastas and fresh pastas that come in many flavors and fun shapes. In this cookbook, you have many sauces to try with pasta dishes. Have fun creating your own! The possibilities are endless!

MAIN KITCHEN TOOLS

People spend so much money on cars, tropical vacations, designer clothes, and dining at fancy restaurants when they could be investing in their health instead. Your health is true wealth. Research and purchase good-quality kitchen appliances to help you easily prepare healthy recipes at home. Remember that you don't necessarily need to purchase the exact tools I use in this book—other products will work just fine, although the results may vary slightly. Choose the products that work best with your budget, cooking goals, and kitchen space.

Juicer. Juicing is a process that extracts water and nutrients from produce (e.g., veggies, greens, and fruits) and separates the fiber or juice pulp. Without the fiber, your digestive system doesn't have to work as hard to break down the food and absorb the nutrients. Organic, freshly made green and vegetable juices are very powerful and healing. Make sure you drink lots of green juices and not just fruit juices.

There are many types of juicers; they are all great, and the one you choose will depend on your individual needs and budget. Do some research to see which type will work best for you. I have a few juicers, but I love my Angel juicer.

Blender. Investing in a good-quality blender is very important because you'll be using your high-speed blender the most while preparing your foods. I love my Vitamix, and I use it many times a day to make smoothies, desserts, flour, sauces, nut cheese, nut milk, and soups, among other things. If you can afford to invest in a Vitamix, I recommend it. Many other companies make great high-speed blenders (e.g.,

Blendtec, Cuisinart, Omega, Ninja, and Breville). Make sure, as with your juicer, that you purchase one that is fast but still gentle on your produce.

Food Processor. Many people think that if they have a blender, they don't need a food processor. You still need a good-quality food processor, as there are some jobs that a blender will not handle.

I use my food processor to make cakes, desserts, and ice cream, as well as to chop veggies, and I can't imagine my life without it. You can use a Vitamix blender for some of these tasks, but for some recipes you'll need a good food processor too. It'll cost you a few pennies, but believe me when I say it's a worthy investment. A good food processor will last you for years. My food processor of choice is Cuisinart. I have a professional one, and it's amazing. I also have a mini food processor, but it's essentially only good for chopping; the motor and bowl capacity won't allow you to do much else.

Dehydrator. A dehydrator uses low temperatures and a fan to dry food. It is essential to have if you are on a raw food diet. The dehydration process allows you to prepare/cook food without destroying the food's life force. You can use it to make raw desserts, cookies, crackers, wraps, chips, pizza, pasta, and many other raw dishes.

It can also be used to warm up foods. There are many different types to choose from, and the one you choose will depend on your budget and how much space you have in your kitchen. I love my Excalibur dehydrator.

If you don't have a dehydrator, you can still create healthy dishes. Just use the lowest setting on your oven and watch your goodies closely. Some of the foods will bake fast, and you don't want them to burn.

Pots and Pans. It is very important to invest in good-quality pots and pans. Choose stoneware, glassware, titanium, stainless steel, cast iron, and clay pots. Avoid aluminum and nonstick Teflon pots. Certain nonstick coatings can become carcinogenic if scratched and heated to high temperatures. Always check with the manufacturer for the product details. I love the Ozeri frying pan for oil-free cooking, such as making pancakes or tofu scramble.

Other Miscellaneous Tools

Here are several more helpful kitchen tools:

- spiralizer for making all kinds of raw pasta (e.g., from zucchini, cucumbers, sweet potatoes, and more)
- mandolin for slicing vegetables thinly, as for making zucchini lasagna and salads
- waffle maker
- coconut opener for opening young Thai coconuts. I have a Coco Jack, and I find it to be the easiest to use, but there are many other options out there.
- cutting board, whether glass or wooden (my preferences) or one of the many other kinds available, all of which will work just fine
- mason jars to store your juice, smoothies, and other foods, such as dry nuts and beans. They come in many shapes, colors, and sizes.
- mixing bowls, preferably made from glass, stainless steel, or porcelain. I try to avoid plastic, but plastic may be the best option for those who have kids.
- sharp knives, particularly stainless steel or ceramic, which are excellent. Good knives are a worthwhile investment.
- peeler for peeling nonorganic produce
- scrub brush for scrubbing potatoes, carrots, and other veggies
- strainers and colanders for rinsing fruit and greens. They are available in stainless steel or plastic, and you can also use them to make nut cheese or sprout nuts and seeds.
- sprouting trays, shelves, jars, or bags to sprout your own seeds and to grow microgreens, nutritionally dense superfoods containing live enzymes and chlorophyll. There are many kinds of sprouting kits to choose from.
- dishes that allow your personality to shine. I collect colorful handmade dishes from around the world. Your choice of dinnerware can greatly influence your presentation of a dish, so have fun with it.
- ice cream maker, of which there are many to choose from, depending on your budget
- nut milk bag for making milk and cheese from nuts
- bamboo sushi rolling mat for making variety of sushi
- popsicle and chocolate molds for making healthy treats

CHAPTER 3

Favorite Ingredients and Substitutions for Vegan Cooking

Cooking is like an art to me, where I create scrumptious delicacies without following specific recipes. Many chefs cook from the heart. They also estimate the measurements. The only time I measure ingredients is when I cook for a class or test recipes for a cookbook. Otherwise, I cook to taste. I experiment with flavors. I taste the food and add spices as needed. This is how I invent my recipes—by combining ingredients most people would find unusual.

COOKING TO TASTE

Most chefs will tell you that even if they use the same ingredients every time they make a dish, it will come out slightly different. One day you may use organic tomatoes from your garden and another day conventional tomatoes from a store, which have not fully ripened yet. The taste of both dishes will be different. Don't just follow the recipe; adjust the ingredients and cook to taste to create mouth-watering dishes.

The following are some of the ingredients I use most often:

- **salts:** pink Himalayan crystal salt, Celtic sea salt, Kalahari Desert salt, Himalayan black salt
- **natural sweeteners:** lucuma powder, mesquite powder, dates, maple syrup, coconut sugar, coconut nectar, unsulphured dried fruits (e.g., apricots, cherries, or figs)
- **sour taste:** lemon juice, lime juice, raw apple cider vinegar, raw coconut vinegar
- **creamy textures:** coconut meat from Thai coconuts or Jamaican coconuts, cashews, macadamia nuts, raw coconut butter, ripe bananas, sun-dried tomatoes
- **cheesy:** nutritional yeast
- **oils:** coconut oil, chia seed oil, hempseed oil, flaxseed oil (These oils are great to use in salad dressings or to add a little flavor to your dish. I also use coconut oil, along with cacao butter and coconut butter, in my raw chocolates.)
- **essential oils:** peppermint, lemon, lavender, orange (My favorite company is Young Living. When using essential oils, make sure they are high quality, therapeutic grade, and made for internal use. You only need a drop or two; otherwise, they may overpower your dish.)
- **fruity flavor:** jackfruit, durian, mango, berries, apples, persimmons
- **dried fruits:** mulberries, figs, dates (look for unsulphured)
- **spices:** turmeric or curry powder, paprika, black pepper, cayenne pepper, Ceylon cinnamon, vanilla (I love the vanilla flavor by Medicine Flower), clove, ginger, cardamom
- **chocolate:** Use raw cacao powder, not cocoa powder. You can also use carob powder.
- **seeds:** chia, hemp, pumpkin, sunflower, buckwheat groats
- **nuts:** walnuts, pecans, hazelnuts, macadamia nuts, Brazil nuts, cashews, pine nuts, pistachios
- **superfoods:** maca, lucuma, mesquite powders, medicinal mushrooms such as reishi and chaga

MEAT SUBSTITUTES

If you have decided to include less meat or leave it out entirely, the following make excellent replacements:

Mushrooms

Grill or bake mushrooms as a substitute for meat. They're great in soups, salads, stews, sauces, meatballs, burgers, pizza, and sandwiches. With their rich and earthy flavor, they can replace meat in any recipe. They go very well with all kinds of vegetables, beans, lentils, and nuts, and are suitable for international dishes. Available in many forms—including fresh, dried, or powdered—mushrooms may be organically grown, locally grown, or wild. Try many different kinds, such as portobello, enoki, morels, chanterelle, boletus, shiitake, and oyster.

Beans and Legumes

There are endless ways to use beans and legumes. In this cookbook, you will find them in many kinds of recipes. A supreme source of protein, they can be used in savory recipes—such as dips, sauces, soups, salads, butters, meatballs, and burgers—or in desserts. They come in many forms, including fresh, dried, canned, or frozen. Try many different varieties, such as black beans, lima beans, chickpeas, mung beans, soybeans, French lentils, red lentils, green lentils, and black lentils.

Jackfruit

Jackfruit is an amazing sweet tropical fruit that grows in Asia. It has a very interesting texture. You can easily use it as a substitute for taco meat, BBQ, pulled pork, or a shepherd's pie; use green for savory dishes. It's great in ethnic dishes, including Thai, Jamaican, Brazilian, Mexican, or Chinese. If you want the jackfruit to be chewier, just roast it on a baking sheet for 15 minutes. Ripe and juicy jackfruit is flavorful by itself.

Tofu

Tofu is made from soybeans and is high in protein and calcium. Originally from Asia, it has been used for ages. Textures include silky, soft, firm, extra firm, or sprouted, and tofu is also available in many flavors, such as BBQ, baked, or spicy. The original flavor by itself is tasteless, so you can add whatever spices or seasoning you wish. Use tofu in soups, stews, sandwiches, quiche, pizza, salads, smoothies, and desserts. Make sure you purchase organic, non-GMO tofu.

jack fruit

Tempeh

Made from fermented soybeans, tempeh has a nutty flavor. It may be fermented with rice, vegetables, or grains to get interesting texture and flavor. It is packed with protein as well as fiber, calcium, and vitamins. Try baking tempeh, marinating it in your favorite sauces, or using it in salads and sandwiches.

Seitan

Seitan, or processed wheat gluten, is a rich source of protein. It has a dense, chewy, meat-like texture that tastes great in many international dishes. Depending on the spices and flavors you use, it can be similar to many dishes made with meat, such as sausages, stews, stir-fry, grilled recipes, sandwiches, or salads. If you tolerate gluten, try seitan to see how closely it imitates meat. I don't use this kind of meat substitute often, but people who are transitioning to a plant-based diet find it very effective in satisfying their meat cravings.

Textured Vegetable Protein (TVP)

TVP is made from dehydrated soy and comes dry in small, medium, or large chunks. Once you rehydrate it, you can use it in soups, stews, burritos, burgers, and more. TVP is very inexpensive, but make sure you buy organic and non-GMO.

GELATIN SUBSTITUTES

The following are natural thickeners you can use in raw or cooked recipes:

- arrowroot powder
- tapioca flour
- agar powder
- Irish moss

Use these substitutes in place of gelatin when making cheese (raw or baked), cakes, cake fillings, and whenever you want to add some extra thickness to your dish. Agar and Irish moss are usually used in raw recipes to maintain their nutritional content. You can purchase them at online health food stores. Arrowroot powder and tapioca flour can be purchased at most grocery stores. Follow the instructions on the package for measuring.

Tip Sheet

EGG SUBSTITUTES FOR BAKING

Baking can be tricky. You need to be very careful and precise when you bake, but even then, your baked goodies may come out slightly different every time you make them. Factors that may affect baking include the following: oven size and type, humidity, and type of ingredients you use (gluten-free flour will bake longer and be denser, for example).

The following are egg substitutes for baking. Each is the equivalent of one egg:

- 1 tablespoon flaxseed meal + 3 tablespoons water (If you don't have flaxseed meal, simply use a coffee grinder to grind flax seeds. Keep in the refrigerator.)
- 1 tablespoon chia seeds + 1 tablespoon water, soaked for 10–20 minutes
- 1 tablespoon applesauce
- 1 tablespoon peanut or almond butter
- 1 tablespoon pumpkin puree
- 1 tablespoon flax seeds + 1–2 tablespoons warm water, soaked for 10 minutes
- 1/2 cup pureed silken tofu
- 1/2 to 1 ripe banana
- 1 teaspoon baking soda + 1 tablespoon white vinegar
- 1/2 teaspoon tapioca flour + 1/2 teaspoon potato flour + 1 tablespoon water

CHAPTER 4

How to Make the Rainbow Diet Easy, Cheesy, Breezy

Try the following ideas for encouraging your whole family to eat healthier:

- **Set an example.** Your children are not going to eat healthy if they see you snacking on junk food.
- **Have healthy food options readily available.** Place chopped veggies and different fruits in small bowls on the counter and offer them as snacks. It is much easier to grab something that is at hand and in sight.
- **Cut fruits and veggies and store them in a container in the refrigerator.** Keep these healthy foods accessible at a level where children can easily see and reach them when they open the fridge.
- **Don't buy junk food.** Resist the urge to buy chips and candy. You can't eat what you don't have.
- **Make healthy treats,** such as fruit popsicles, desserts, smoothies, raw chocolate, veggie pizza, and raw pasta.
- **Introduce healthy wraps,** such as kale, lettuce, or collard greens, instead of tortillas.
- **Bake French fries** instead of frying. Even better, make sweet potatoes baked fries.
- **Dehydrate or bake your own chips,** such as banana, sweet potato, apple, zucchini, beet, carrot, and mango.
- **Drink infused water** with fruit, veggies, and herbs.
- **Drink herbal coffee** like Teeccino instead of regular coffee.
- **Try cocktail recipes** from **"Nature's Gifts From the Bar" (Chapter 15)** instead of alcoholic drinks.
- **Have a smoothie** instead of a cake.
- **Use sugar alternatives** like SUGAR 2.0, coconut sugar, date sugar, monk-fruit sugar, dates, or ripe bananas instead of white sugar.
- **Make food from scratch.** Avoid microwaving pre-packaged frozen food.
- **When dining out,** order a salad, soup, and lots of veggies. Make the salad more filling by asking for a baked potato or quinoa on a side.
- **When traveling or going to work,** always carry a healthy snack with you, such as dates, nuts, or dried fruit. Reach for them when you need an energy-boost during the day, are stuck in the office a little longer, or sitting in traffic.
- **Carry water** with you to work and throughout the day.

Remember, it takes about twenty times for the taste buds to get used to a new flavor, so don't get discouraged. Keep introducing new, healthy recipes. You can use these methods with your spouse, children, and anybody who needs to eat healthier. If I don't offer my husband a healthy snack or fruit, he will not take it by himself.

The following are more strategies for making the transition into a rainbow plant-based diet easier and more fun. Try these tricks:

• Try something new every day. Don't judge the food by its looks. You may be surprised by how delicious that ethnic, plant-based dish can be.

• If you don't like a particular vegetable in its raw state, try sautéing it or cooking it in a soup.

• Season your food with spices and herbs. Fresh herbs can greatly enhance food's natural flavor. Use fresh or dried herbs and spices to make your palate happy.

• Participate in cookouts. Gather with your neighbors, friends, or colleagues to share your recipes. Discover a healthy alternative to a common dish. Taste something exotic. Be inspired by the way your backyard neighbor used dairy-free cream instead of mayo in a potato salad. Possibilities are endless if you are open to new options and allow yourself to enjoy the culinary adventure.

• Pretend that you are a child, and play and experiment with food. Yes, play with food, although your mom always told you otherwise. Make your life fun and playful in the kitchen. Happiness starts in your stomach.

• Take a cooking class, and consult a health coach or a nutritionist.

• Educate yourself about domestic or international health retreats, cruises, and detox programs, etc.

FOOD ART FOR KIDS

Make food-preparation time fun for the whole family. Here are some tips to help you engage your children and get creative in a kitchen:

• Make fun pizza shapes. Try **Butternut Squash Pizza Lovers' Pizzas** (see recipe page 177).

• Use cookie cutters to cut out fun shapes for cookies, sandwiches, and snacks.

• Make smoothie bowls. Sprinkle them with **Unicorn Rainbow Magical Sprinkles** (see recipe page 148), and decorate with fun shapes of cutout fruit.

• Make colorful popsicles, fruit rollups, and ice cream.

• Cook and bake at home. Make healthy cookies, cupcakes, and donuts. Decorate them with natural frosting made of banana ice cream or cashew cream.

• When baking muffins, press them with another

muffin pan halfway through to create sunken tops. Serve with banana ice cream, cashew frosting, or cashew cream.

• Go to the forest to pick wild blueberries.

• Take your children food shopping; go to a farm to pick your own apples, pumpkins, strawberries, etc. I have been going to the Lawrence Farm Orchard in Newburgh, New York, for over eighteen years, and I always get inspired by nature.

• Getting the entire family involved will make cooking fast and easy. Your children can help you make their favorite dinner, set the table, and do the dishes.

• Let your children have their own garden and grow herbs or sprouts.

• Take a cooking class together.

• Let your creativity shine. Experiment with new dishes, and you and your children will develop new plant-based cooking skills in no time.

• The perfect way to create delicious food is to use simple, fresh, natural ingredients. Add new, exciting flavors and fun to your cooking, such as edible flowers, spices, and herbs.

• Go to an ethnic food store to get inspired by exotic flavors. Pick a new fruit or vegetable every time you go there, and ask your children to create a new recipe.

• Get inspired by the shapes and colors of nature.

• Let your imagination shine!

Tip Sheet

AFFORDING A PLANT-BASED DIET ON A BUDGET

Eating healthy doesn't have to cost a lot. The following strategies can help:

FRESH IS BEST! Buy fresh produce, dry beans, and legumes directly from local farmers. I use Mike's Organic delivery service to have fresh, locally grown produce delivered to my door every week.

BUY IN BULK FROM LOCAL FOOD STORES OR ONLINE. You and your friends can split up the cost every week. It is so much cheaper when you buy in bulk.

START AN ORGANIC GARDEN. In the summertime, grow veggies and herbs outside; in the winter months, grow herbs in pots inside. Learn how to sprout nuts, seeds, and grains.

DON'T THROW RIPE FRUITS AWAY. Instead, save money by getting creative. Use ripe fruits to make fruit rollups, popsicles, raw cake, or ice cream (see recipes in Chapters 5, 8, 13). Cube ripe fruits and veggies, and freeze in a glass container for later.

INVEST IN A DEHYDRATOR (choose the one that fits your budget) so you can make your own healthy treats instead of buying expensive ones.

CHAPTER 5

Here's To Life: Let's Raise Our Glasses With Happy Juice!

Drinking juice every day is the best thing you can do for your health. Try to incorporate green juice into your diet, not just fruit juice. Nothing is more nutritious than green juice. Green juices contain high levels of chlorophyll, a powerful phytonutrient. Green plants help us detox, provide necessary nutrients, and give us sustainable energy that lasts for hours. Green symbolizes the energy of love, vitality, compassion, life, joy, nature, balance, peace, and transformation. Green juice is simply a blood-life force of plants. Did you know that juice gets absorbed into our system in just fifteen minutes? So juice up and stay healthy and energized!

You can choose any combination of juice recipes in this book for your one-day detox. To make any delicious juice from the selection below, process all ingredients in a juicer. Serve immediately or store in a glass jar for up to twenty-four hours.

TURN UP THE BEET

3 beets
3 carrots
1 green apple

GOOD MORNING SUNSHINE

1 fennel bulb
1 green apple
3 stalks celery
1 lemon
1 handful spinach
1 inch fresh ginger root

PINK LADY

4 pink grapefruits
1 lemon
1 apple
1 cucumber
1/2 cup raspberries

TROPICAL PARADISE

1/2 pineapple
1 lemon
1 lime
1 orange
1 grapefruit
You can drink it like this or add 1 cup fresh raw coconut water.

GREEN HEALTH MACHINE

5 leaves Swiss chard
5 leaves kale
1 cucumber
1 lemon
1 green apple
1 bunch parsley
3 stalks celery
1 zucchini
thumbnail jalapeño pepper (optional)

Juice with Polish Pickles
by Patrycja Żuchowska (Poland)

Patrycja Żuchowska was born in Poland, where she grew up watching her grandmother make cucumbers in brine every summer. Ever since her grandma passed away, Patrycja has been continuing the tradition.

Today, Patrycja is a registered nurse in a busy cardiovascular unit. Every day, she is reminded of the importance of good, healthy nutrition and daily physical activity. Patrycja has made Pennsylvania her home and is dedicated to helping people make the right choices regarding nutrition and exercise.

5 ripe tomatoes
4–5 celery stalks
3–4 homemade **Pick Me Up Polish Pickles (see recipe page 101)**, plus brine for adding to finished juice
3–4 leaves kale
2–3 red bell peppers (you can use green, orange, or yellow)
2–3 beets
2–3 carrots
1–2 inches fresh ginger
1 fennel
1 jalapeňo pepper (optional)
celeriac

DIRECTIONS:
Process all ingredients in a juicer. Add a tablespoon of brine, or more to taste, to finished juice.

SKINNY ZUCCHINI MARTINI
2 zucchini
1 pear
1 sweet potato
1 lime
1/4 small purple cabbage
1-inch ginger root

SWEET POTATO PIE
3 sweet potatoes
2 apples
1 orange
1 lemon
1/4 pineapple
1-inch ginger root
1-inch turmeric root
cinnamon powder, for sprinkling on top

WATERMELON BLUEBERRY ICE-CREAM FLOAT
5 cups cubed watermelon
1 lemon
1 small cucumber
a few leaves fresh mint
Ice cream:
3 frozen ripe bananas
1/2 cup frozen blueberries

DIRECTIONS:
1. Mix juice ingredients in a high-speed blender.
2. Mix ice cream ingredients separately in a high-speed blender.
3. Serve juice over ice cream in a tall glass.

Jackie's Favorite Juices

Jackie O'Reilly is a mother of three small children. She was raised on a conventional American diet and lifestyle. Throughout her life, she suffered from various chronic inflammatory health conditions and hormonal problems. To improve her health, she started replacing her processed, conventional diet with all natural, whole, organic foods. She has been on a raw food diet since November 2014 and is happy to announce that she has lost seventy-three pounds and is off all medications.

She credits juice fasting for her successful weight-loss transformation. Her children are on a mostly raw diet, and they are very healthy as well. Her favorite part about this lifestyle is that she didn't have to give up chocolate (raw cacao). www.jackieloydsfb.wix.com/mysite

LIME AIDE JUICE

2 limes
2 cucumbers
2 cups baby spinach
1 apple

TROPICAL DREAM JUICE

1 or 2 pints blueberries
2 star fruits
1/4 or 1/2 pineapple
fresh coconut water (optional)

DELIGHTFUL DANDELION JUICE

2 cups dandelion leaves
3 oranges
3 red apples
1 lemon

UNICORN JUICE

1 pomegranate
1 orange
1 star fruit
1 kiwi
1 cup baby spinach
1/2 cup blueberries or blackberries
1/2 cup grapes

SOUR GREEN JUICE

1 head Romaine lettuce
2 green apples
1 lime
1 bunch cilantro

MINT CUCUMBER COOLER

3 large cucumbers
3 green apples
bunch fresh mint

CHAPTER 6

Make Your Life Frothy: I Drink Tea; You Drink Coffee

Populations have used coffee and tea for centuries. Tea has less caffeine than coffee. It contains a lot of antioxidants and can improve your health. There are many different kinds of tea, such as green, oolong, white, rooibos, herbal, fruit, and black. You can drink it hot or cold. My favorite teas are coconut oolong, jasmine green tea, holy basil, lavender, peppermint, and rooibos. Peppermint and ginger tea will soothe your stomach and help with digestion. Lavender and chamomile will help you relax and unwind.

Experiment with different kinds of tea and find your favorite, but opt for organic varieties if possible to avoid pesticides. Visit your local health food store for a variety of tea flavors; make your own tea by adding dried or fresh fruit, spices, and herbs; and consult a naturopath to find out about tea properties. If you want to find out more about tea, visit the websites listed in the back of the book.

As a health coach, my clients always ask me if coffee is good for them. It depends on many factors. There is a difference between drinking coffee because you enjoy the taste and drinking it because you have to. An occasional cup of coffee once in a while or even once a day is fine, but if you need coffee to wake up, and then more cups throughout the day to keep going, you are obviously addicted to caffeine. If that's the case, you could try walking, exercising, getting more rest, using essential oils, or drinking more water to give you energy. There are many superfoods that will boost your energy level, such as moringa, ginseng, or matcha green tea. Also, conventionally produced coffee is heavily sprayed with pesticides, so opt for organic coffee if possible.

If you would like to get off caffeine or reduce your intake, I recommend herbal coffee. You can find many kinds of herbal coffee in health food stores. Many of these coffees are made of chaga mushrooms, chicory root, Israeli artichoke, or roasted grains. Some are instant and some are ground. You can choose from Teeccino, Four Sigmatic, Dandi Blend, or Kawa Inka/Cafmix. Kawa Inka is very popular in Poland. I used to drink it as a child.

To make the transition easier, first add a small amount of herbal coffee to your regular coffee. The next day, increase the amount of herbal coffee and decrease the regular coffee. Continue in this manner until you are ready to drink herbal coffee only. It doesn't have the exact smell or taste of regular coffee, but it comes close, and you can add your favorite nut creamer or nut milk, such as coconut, cashew, almond, or soy.

Heart Healing Tea

by Deb Miller (Australia)

Deb Miller loves exploring and learning about personal and planetary healing and evolution through the physical and spiritual worlds. She lives in Australia and trained in the 1980s to be an herbalist. Since then, she has studied and worked as a massage therapist, aromatherapist, spiritual and energetic healer, and naturopath.

Herbs have a consciousness that helps people to grow and change on a mental, emotional, and spiritual level, not only physical. This Heart Healing blend assists with healing heartbreak, grief, sadness, loss, rejection, and betrayal. She offers it from her heart to yours. Visit Deb at her website, www.sourcesessencehealing.com.au or on Instagram @sourceessencehealing. You can also e-mail her at deb@sourceessence.com.au

Serves 1
1 teaspoon dried hawthorn berries/blossoms
1 teaspoon dried rose petals
1 teaspoon dried rose hips
coconut sugar, for sweetening

DIRECTIONS:
1. Infuse the herbs in 1 cup of boiled water for 5 minutes, or longer if you like it stronger. Do not infuse it too long, as it could become bitter.
2. Add some coconut sugar to taste if needed.
3. Drink three times a day for emotional healing.

CREAMY MATCHA LATTE
by Lidia Bis

Serves 1–2
1–2 Medjool dates, pitted
1 1/2 cups cold filtered water
1 tablespoon raw cashews
1 tablespoon hemp seeds
1 tablespoon matcha green tea

Place all ingredients in a high-speed blender and mix until smooth.

BABY, IT'S COLD OUTSIDE HOT CHOCOLATE
by Lyndi Caruso

Lyndi Caruso lives in Maryland on an urban farmette with chickens, horses, dogs, and a tortoise. She loves the simple things in life: good food, good friends, and the outdoors. She is passionate about health, nutrition, and horses, and she is knowledgeable about Young Living essential oils.
www.lyndislifestyle.com

Serves 1
2–4 Medjool dates, pitted, or 1/4 cup maple syrup
1/4 cup raw cashews
1–2 tablespoons cacao
2 ounces coconut milk or 1 tablespoon coconut oil
8 ounces hot water

DIRECTIONS:
1. Place all ingredients in a blender and blend until rich and creamy, or let it go a little longer for the latte effect.
2. Savor in your favorite cup with a sprinkle of fresh ground cinnamon or nutmeg.

VARIATION: Experiment with your favorite flavors and add cinnamon, nutmeg, cardamom, clove, black pepper, cayenne pepper, vanilla, orange zest, fresh ginger, maca powder, moringa, matcha powder, spirulina, or a few drops of therapeutic-grade essential oils.

RASPBERRY GARDEN TEA
by Daria Jabenko (Russia)

Daria Jabenko is a chic brand designer. Originally from Moscow, Russia, she has for many years resided in Toronto, Canada. Drawing with watercolors has been Daria's passion since she can remember. She spent years illustrating and making award winning animations for Cosmopolitan, Elle, Madame, Condé Nast Germany, Hallmark, and Papyrus, to name a few. She has incorporated all this experience into chic branding for women entrepreneurs by creating custom, hand-drawn animations and branding packages. It's time for women to share their messages and make their messages irresistible. www.misschicnbeautiful.com

Serves 1-2
6 fresh mint leaves
3 1/2 ounces fresh raspberries
1 cinnamon stick
coconut sugar or agave nectar to taste

DIRECTIONS:
1. Wash mint leaves in cold water.
2. Put mint leaves in a transparent glass teapot (so that you can admire the beauty of this tea).
3. Boil 2 cups water and pour over the leaves in the teapot. Cover with lid and wait for 5 minutes.
4. Add raspberries and wait 10 minutes.
5. Add cinnamon stick and coconut sugar before serving.

WHEN COWS FLY NUT MILK

1 cup raw, unsalted cashews
2–3 cups water, depending on whether you want it creamy or not

DIRECTIONS:
1. Combine cashews and water in a high-speed blender and blend until smooth (cashews are soft nuts and do not require soaking).
2. Using a piece of muslin or a nut milk bag, squeeze out the liquid.
3. Store in a mason jar in a refrigerator for about 3 days.

VARIATIONS: Use different kinds of nuts or seeds, such as Brazil nuts, macadamia nuts, hazelnuts, walnuts, almonds, sunflower seeds, or hemp seeds. Soaking time will vary depending on the kind of nuts you are using.

For a sweeter taste, add a sweetener of your choice, such as dates, coconut sugar, maple syrup, agave, etc.

To create flavored nut milk, add vanilla, raw cacao, carob powder, matcha powder, or fruit.

GOLDEN TURMERIC MILK
Try this warm drink before bedtime to help you relax and unwind.

Serves 1-2
2 cups nut milk (almond, coconut, or cashew)
1 teaspoon turmeric powder or 1-inch fresh turmeric
1 teaspoon maple syrup, raw coconut nectar, or coconut sugar (or more if you like a sweeter taste)
1/2 teaspoon Ceylon cinnamon
tiny piece fresh peeled ginger root or 1/4 teaspoon ginger powder
pinch black pepper (increases absorption)
pinch cardamom
pinch cayenne pepper (optional)

DIRECTIONS:
1. Blend all ingredients in a high-speed blender until smooth.
2. Pour mixture into a small saucepan. Heat for 3–5 minutes over medium heat until hot but not boiling. Serve immediately.

VARIATION: Instead of spices, use 1/2 to 1 teaspoon **Pumpkin Spice (see recipe page 106)**, plus the fresh ginger.

Jamaican Mocha Teccino

(raw/gluten-free)

Teeccino is a healthy, caffeine-free, herbal alternative to regular coffee.
This version was inspired by my trip to Jamaica.

Serves 1–2

2 bags mocha or hazelnut Teeccino

3 Medjool dates, pitted

2 ripe bananas, frozen

1/2 cup almond milk

1 tablespoon raw cacao powder

1 tablespoon raw coconut cream or meat from
fresh coconut

1/2 teaspoon reishi powder (optional)

pinch pink Himalayan salt

pinch Ceylon cinnamon

cayenne pepper to taste

shredded coconut flakes, for garnish

DIRECTIONS:

1. Steep Teeccino bags in 1 cup hot water and leave to cool.

2. Add the remaining ingredients except shredded coconut flakes to a high-speed blender and blend. Add ice if you want an extra-chilled smoothie.

3. Top with shredded coconut and serve.

VARIATION: Top it off with whipped coconut cream or banana ice cream for a rich dessert.

CHAPTER 7

Let's Get Fruity!

Many people worry about eating more fruit, fearing it has too much sugar. But there is a difference between sugar that comes in natural form and processed sugar. When you eat sugar in its natural state, like the sugar in fruit, your body assimilates it in a way that is beneficial to you. It's processed sugar or white sugar that should be avoided at all costs.

If you have a health condition and follow a low-sugar diet, there are certain vegetables that are high in sugar you may want to avoid. Eat plenty of leafy greens instead. Be cautious, too, of sugary fruits like apricots, mangos, melons, papayas, prunes, and pineapples. Listen to your body, and consult a health practitioner to help you decide which foods are right for you.

Include plenty of the following fruits and vegetables in your diet: avocados, bell peppers, cucumbers, tomatoes, zucchinis, squash, pumpkins, eggplants, lemons, limes, and berries.

No one has ever said,
"I've eaten too many apples today."
– Aleksandra Winters

MAKING FOOD COLORFUL

My recipes are very colorful, as you'll see throughout this book. Here are some quick tips for achieving rainbow-colored recipes using natural ingredients:

RED — beets (or beet powder), goji berries, cranberries, raspberries, cherries, watermelon, strawberries, hibiscus tea

ORANGE — carrots (or carrot powder), sweet potatoes, oranges, pumpkins, mix of red and yellow foods/ingredients

YELLOW — pineapples, mangos, corn, saffron, turmeric powder

GREEN — spinach, avocado, spirulina, chlorella, wheatgrass, moringa, green matcha powder, mix of blue and yellow foods/ingredients

PURPLE — purple cabbage, beetroot powder, purple grapes, blueberries, blackberries, maqui berry powder, mix of red and blue foods/ ingredients

WHITE — coconut meat or shredded coconut, cashews, bananas (use also to lighten other colors— e.g., mix with purple to make lavender or red to make pink)

BLUE — Blue coloring is the hardest to make. Yes, blueberries are blue, but when you mix them, you will get a purple color. To achieve a beautiful blue color, I use E3Live Blue Majik powder or Thai Butterfly Pea Blue Flower tea.

HOT PINK — pink dragon fruit (pitaya), pink cactus fruit

These are just some examples; the possibilities are endless. Mixing your own colors is like painting and inventing your own color palette. Just have fun and experiment with natural pigments in the kitchen. Remember that when you add something acidic, like lime or lemon juice, your color will change too.

CHAPTER 8
To Smoothie or Not to Smoothie?

Smoothies are fast and easy to make. They are excellent for breakfast, lunch, or dessert. Make sure to include lots of juices and smoothies in your diet. Visit a local health food store or a farmers' market for a variety of fresh produce. I use a local delivery service called Mike's Organic Delivery, and every week I get local, organic produce delivered to my door.

Avoid making smoothies with fruit only. Add a variety of greens—such as spinach, kale, and dandelion leaves—which contain lots of chlorophyll. The more raw food you eat, the better your overall health will be because the food has retained more of its essential nutrients. You can choose any combination of the smoothies and juices in this book for your one-day detox.

To make any delicious smoothie from the selection below, follow these directions: Combine all ingredients and blend in a high-speed blender until smooth. Adjust thickness to your taste by adding more filtered water, coconut water, juice, or nut milk.

WARRIOR SMOOTHIE

2 ripe bananas
2-3 Medjool dates, pitted
1 cup raw coconut water
2 tablespoons raw cacao powder
2 tablespoons chia seeds
1 tablespoon maca powder
ice (optional)

KALE WILL NOT FAIL

4-5 leaves kale
3 ripe bananas
1 cup wild, fresh, or frozen blueberries
1 cup coconut water or filtered water

I AM A HOT SMOOTHIE MACHINE

2 ripe bananas, frozen
1 mango
1/4 pineapple, cubed
1 ripe peach
1 cup spinach or kale
1 cup coconut water

ABC SMOOTHIE

2 apples
2 ripe bananas
2 stalks celery

KEEP IT CLEAN SMOOTHIE

2 ripe bananas
1 ripe persimmon
1 small cucumber
1 carrot
1 orange, peeled
juice of 1/2 lemon
1 cup spinach
1-inch fresh ginger

SPRING IS HERE PIÑA COLADA SMOOTHIE

1/2 ripe pineapple, cubed
4 ripe bananas, fresh or frozen
1 1/2 cups water or coconut water
1 cup young dandelion leaves (or spinach)
1-2 tablespoons coconut butter
1-inch raw turmeric root

Miami Fruit
by Edelle and Rane

Rane Roatta and Edelle Schlegel are fruit-lovers and green-living enthusiasts. They work on a beautiful tropical MiamiFruit farm. MiamiFruit is a Miami-based fruit hub created by Rane to make tropical fruits accessible to people all over the United States. They sell delicious and exotic fruits, such as mamey, jackfruit, black sapote, jaboticaba, sapodilla, canistel, and all kinds of rare bananas. As fruit-loving vegans who care about how food tastes, they make sure they go above and beyond normal standards to have the best-quality fruit. They are also into growing rare fruits, such as soursop, abiu, and rollinia.
www.miamifruit.com

MAMEY SPICE PIE SMOOTHIE

3 1/2 cups frozen mamey
3 1/2 cups water
1 cup almond milk, unsweetened
1 frozen banana
4 Medjool dates, pitted
1 teaspoon cinnamon
dash nutmeg
dash cloves
dash ginger

CHOCOLATE PUDDING FRUIT SMOOTHIE

3 frozen bananas
3 cups frozen black sapote
2 cups water
2 cups almond milk, unsweetened
1 teaspoon cacao
2 walnuts
1 Brazil nut

SEASONAL DELIGHT
by Sofia Bojaj and Ana Lise Devery

This recipe was created by Sofia Bojaj and Ana Lise Devery. Ana and Sofia were art students of Mrs. Winters. To make this smoothie, Sofia and Ana mixed their favorite fruit together with ice and juice, inspired by Mrs. Winters' first cookbook, *Raw Food Art: Four Seasons of Plant-Powered Goodness*. They had to test it a few times to create a perfect smoothie. Sofia and Ana Lise had a lot of fun making the smoothie and hope that you will too. This is a healthy drink to have at any time.

Serves 2
2 cups blueberries
2 cups orange juice, freshly squeezed
1 cup strawberries, sliced
1 cup banana, sliced

GINGER IN THE GRASS
by Shane Stuart

Shane Stuart's dream of enhancing people's lives through changing their nutritional habits materialized when he opened his first Grass Roots juice bar in 2014. Through Grass Roots, he has formed cohesive relationships with small regional farms. Shane is a co-owner of a cutting-edge health, wellness, and learning center named Panacea. Located in Las Vegas Boca Park of the Summerlin community, Panacea includes an organic juice bar, wellness center, plant-based restaurant, and elixir bar, creating a hub for health-conscious consumers, wellness-seekers, and foodies.
www.panacealv.com
@rawmixologist

Makes 24 ouces
1 cup green grapes
1 cup spinach
1/2 cup pineapple
1/2 cup ice
1/4 lemon with skin
thumbnail ginger

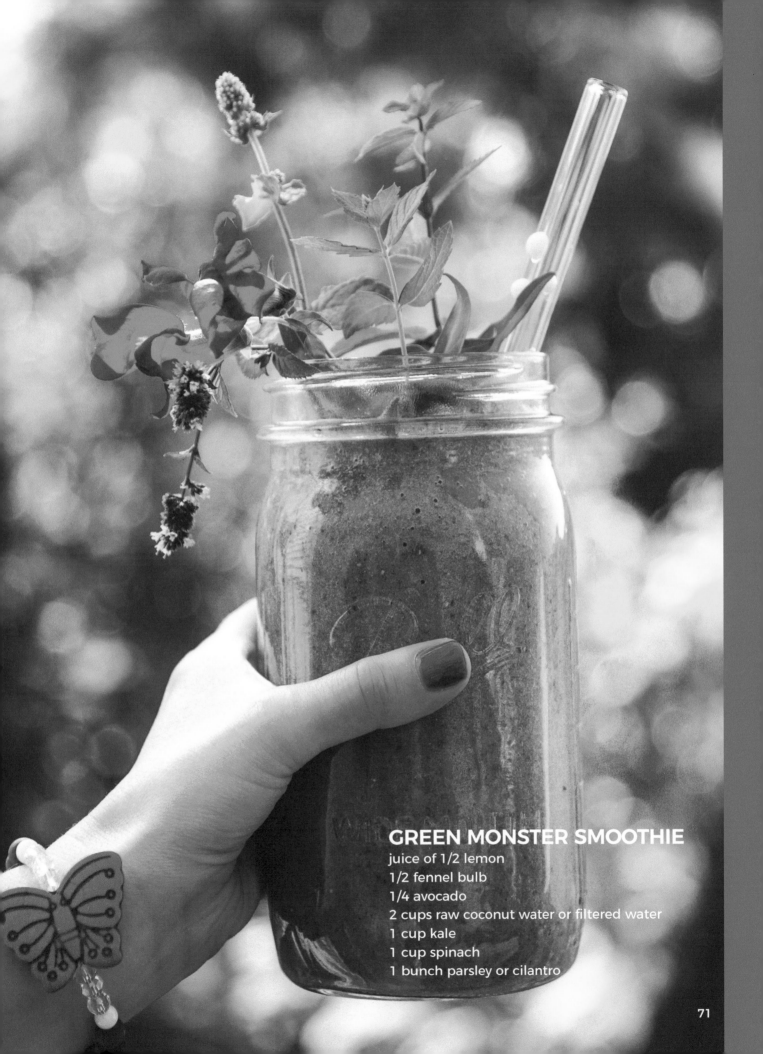

GREEN MONSTER SMOOTHIE

juice of 1/2 lemon
1/2 fennel bulb
1/4 avocado
2 cups raw coconut water or filtered water
1 cup kale
1 cup spinach
1 bunch parsley or cilantro

Food Is My Life. Would You Share It with Me? I Will Make You a Scrumptious Breakfast.

RISE AND SHINE; THAT BREAKFAST BURRITO IS MINE

Serves 1–2

1 small onion, chopped

1 small bell pepper, chopped

1/2 teaspoon turmeric

1/2 curry powder

8 ounces mushrooms, chopped

14 ounces firm tofu (you may use soft)

salt and pepper to taste

3 cups cooked **Steaming Quinoa (see recipe page 167)**

parsley or cilantro

tortilla wraps

Guac N Roll (see recipe page 101)

Mexican salsa

DIRECTIONS:

1. In a pan, combine onion, pepper, turmeric, curry, and 1/2–1 cup water. Cover and cook until soft.
2. Add mushrooms and cook for additional 2–3 minutes.
3. Drain the water from tofu. Place tofu in a bowl and crumble with a fork. Add to pan and cook for another 2–3 minutes. Season with salt and pepper.
4. Transfer mixture to a big bowl. Add quinoa and mix. Garnish with parsley or cilantro.
5. Wrap mixture in a tortilla. Serve with guacamole and salsa.

VARIATIONS: Add spinach, tomatoes, asparagus, coconut aminos, sriracha, salsa, and/or **Not Your Mom's Mozzarella (see recipe page 87).**

  • Use raw coconut wraps or collard greens in place of tortillas.

Brazilian Açaí Bowl

by Ana Sandee (Brazil)

Ana Sandee is a proud Brazilian American, professional foodie, excited home chef, world traveler, and culinary thrill-seeker who has recently added mommy-hood to her résumé. She is an avid health and wellness promoter who travels the world seeking inspiration to develop healthier versions of recipes without sacrificing the taste of delicious food. This recipe is inspired by her Brazilian heritage.
www.colorfulfoodie.com

Serves 1 (raw/gluten-free)

BOWL:
1 cup strawberries, frozen
1 banana
1 ounce coconut meat
1 açaí pack, frozen
a little bit of water or coconut water to get blender going

TOPPINGS: granola, more strawberries or other berries that you have at hand, banana slices, shredded coconut, a drizzle of agave, maple syrup, or coconut nectar

DIRECTIONS:
1. Blend all ingredients in a high-speed blender.
2. Drink as a smoothie or add to a bowl. Sprinkle with toppings and enjoy for breakfast.

OOH LA LA CHIA PUDDING
(raw/gluten-free)

Serves 1–2

3 tablespoons chia seeds
1 cup filtered water
1 cup **When Cows Fly Nut Milk (see recipe page 61)**
fruit for serving: berries, mango, sliced bananas, persimmons, or dried cranberries
cinnamon

DIRECTIONS:
1. In a large bowl, mix chia seeds with water and let sit for about 10–20 minutes.
2. Add nut milk (with or without the pulp).
3. Serve with fruit and sprinkle cinnamon on top.

VARIATION: Add some oats and raw buckwheat sprouts for a different texture.

COCONUT RICE PUDDING (gluten-free)

Serves 6–8
5-6 ripe bananas, frozen
5 Medjool dates, pitted, or dried figs
1/2 cup almond or coconut milk
1–2 tablespoons raw coconut butter
pinch cinnamon
pinch vanilla
2–3 cups brown rice, cooked (or any rice of your choice)

DIRECTIONS:
1. Blend all ingredients except rice in a high-speed blender.
2. Pour over rice. Serve with toppings of your choice.

VARIATION: Other possible toppings include dry mulberries, strawberries, blueberries, raspberries, mango, shredded coconut, cacao nibs, or cinnamon.
 • Serve the pudding with just coconut milk and fruit without the frozen bananas. It's like a healthy milk soup for breakfast.
 • Use quinoa, teff, or steel oats instead of rice.

FOUR SPICE SISTERS BANANA RICE (gluten-free)

Serves 6–8
Rice:
3 cups brown rice, cooked
1/4 teaspoon ginger powder
1/4 teaspoon cardamom powder
1/4 teaspoon nutmeg powder
12–15 very ripe bananas
1 teaspoon Ceylon cinnamon

Sauce:
10 ripe bananas, frozen
7–10 Medjool dates, pitted
4–5 tablespoons raw coconut cream
1 cup raw coconut water or filtered water
1/4 teaspoon vanilla powder or 1/2 teaspoon Medicine Flower vanilla
pinch cinnamon

DIRECTIONS:
1. Make rice: In a big bowl, mix rice with ginger, cardamom, and nutmeg and transfer to a glass or ceramic baking dish. Cover with 1 cup of pure water. Slice bananas and put over rice. Sprinkle with cinnamon. Bake for 50–60 minutes in a preheated oven at 350°F.
2. Make sauce: Mix sauce ingredients in a high-speed blender.
3. Serve rice warm or cold, topped with sauce.

VARIATION: Serve as a dessert or breakfast. Add the topping of your choice: apples, mangos, pears, bananas, dry mulberries, dates, prunes, peaches, plums, berries, cacao nibs, walnuts, other nuts, etc.

SPRINKLE SPRINKLE LITTLE STAR SUPERFOOD MOONLIGHT GRANOLA

Serves 4-6

1/2 cup maple syrup or coconut nectar
juice of 1/2 lemon
1 tablespoon pumpkin spice (cinnamon, cardamom, ginger, nutmeg)
1/2 teaspoon cinnamon
1/2 teaspoon vanilla
coconut oil
2 cups gluten-free oats
1 cup pumpkin seeds
1 cup cranberries
1 cup sliced almonds
1/2 cup sunflower seeds
1/2 cup raisins
1/2 cup mulberries
1/2 cup shredded coconut

DIRECTIONS:

1. Preheat oven to 350°F.
2. In a small bowl, combine syrup, lemon juice, pumpkin spice, cinnamon, and vanilla.
3. Grease a baking sheet with coconut oil or use parchment paper. Place the remaining ingredients on the sheet.
4. Pour the maple syrup mixture over the loose ingredients.
5. Bake for an hour. Stir once halfway through.
6. Serve immediately or store in a glass jar for several weeks.

VARIATION: Serve with nut milk, vegan yogurt, or fruits like bananas, mangos, berries, figs, pineapple, and apples. You can decorate it with fresh herbs and **Unicorn Rainbow Magical Sprinkles (see recipe page 148).**

WATERMELON PIZZA
(raw/gluten-free)

Serves 6–8

medium watermelon
Toppings:
oranges, strawberries, raspberries, blueberries,
bananas, star fruit, nuts, basil, mint, Unicorn
Rainbow Magical Sprinkles (see recipe page 148)

DIRECTIONS:

Cut watermelon into round slices.
Cut each round slice into four parts/triangles.

Top the watermelon "pizza" slice with toppings
of your choice.

Happy Yummy In My Tummy Crispy Waffles

Serves 4–6

Waffles:

1 ripe banana

1 cup oat flour

1 cup millet flour

1/2 cup oats

2 tablespoons maple syrup

2 tablespoons flaxseed meal or chia seeds

1 tablespoon pure vanilla extract

1 1/2 teaspoons aluminum-free baking powder

1 teaspoon raw apple cider vinegar (optional)

1/2 teaspoon pumpkin spice

1 1/2 cups almond or coconut milk

Toppings:

seasonal fruits

edible flowers

maple syrup

You May Be Surprised, But This Ice Cream Tastes So Nice (see recipe page 131)

DIRECTIONS:

1. In a big mixing bowl, mash the banana with a fork, and then add remaining waffle ingredients, leaving the almond milk for last.

2. Mix the batter and pour into a waffle maker. When waffles are ready, decorate with seasonal fruits and edible flowers and serve with syrup and/or ice cream.

VARIATIONS: Use just oat, millet, or buckwheat flour, or any other gluten-free flour.

• Sprinkle some **Unicorn Rainbow Magical Sprinkles** on top **(see recipe page 148)**.

• If you want to make your waffles colorful, mix raw spinach with the milk in a high-speed blender for green color, raspberries or beet powder for red, turmeric for yellow, and blueberries for purple. **Use Olenko's natural color guide/Making Food Colorful (see page 67)** for natural food coloring.

• If you want your waffles to be crispy, add raw apple cider vinegar at the end.

Sparkle of Magic Overnight Oats

(raw)

Serves 1–2

Oatmeal:

2 cups of your favorite dairy-free milk (cashew, coconut, almond, rice, soy, etc.)

1 tablespoon chia seeds

1 cup gluten-free rolled oats (add more or use less depending on how thick you like your overnight oats)

Toppings:

2–3 tablespoons goji berries

2–3 tablespoons raisins or mulberries

1 tablespoon sunflower or pumpkin seeds

pinch of your favorite spices (ginger, cinnamon, turmeric, or vanilla)

DIRECTIONS:

1. In a mason jar or a bowl, combine milk, chia seeds, and oats. Stir until oats and seeds are immersed in milk and mixed well. Cover with a lid and refrigerate overnight (or for at least 4–6 hours so flavors can combine).

2. The next day, add your favorite toppings. If the oats are too thick, add more milk.

3. Serve from a jar or transfer to a bowl. You can bring them to work, school, or a picnic. Overnight oats will keep in a refrigerator for up to 2 days.

VARIATIONS: Add maple syrup or coconut sugar if you like a sweeter taste.

• Other possible toppings include sliced banana, strawberries, raspberries, blueberries, mangos, peaches, persimmons, dates, hemp or flax seeds, peanut or almond butter, walnuts, hazelnuts, pecans, **Unicorn Rainbow Magical Sprinkles (see recipe page 148)**, **Sprinkle Sprinkle Little Star Superfood Moonlight Granola (see recipe page 75)**, or your favorite smoothie.

Perfect Pancakes for Smiley Days

(gluten-free)

My husband, Bill, loves these light and fluffy pancakes. You can add other fruits—such as blueberries—or raw cacao powder to create different flavors. You can also use this recipe to make buckwheat waffles.

Serves 8–10

2 ripe bananas

2 cups buckwheat flour

1 1/2 cups coconut milk or nut milk of your choice

1 teaspoon baking powder

1 teaspoon chia seeds (optional)

1/2 teaspoon cinnamon

extra virgin coconut oil

maple syrup and fresh fruits, for serving

DIRECTIONS:

1. Mash bananas with a fork.
2. In a mixing bowl, combine bananas with flour, coconut milk, 1/2 cup water, baking powder, chia seeds (if using), and cinnamon. Mix well until lumps disappear. Add more milk or water if needed.
3. Ladle pancake batter onto a heated pan lightly greased with extra virgin coconut oil. Cook until golden brown and flip over.
4. Serve with maple syrup and your favorite fruits.

CHAPTER 10

Leave the Past in the Past and Go Nuts for Nutty and Cheesy Side Dishes

Whether you like crunchy, salty, spicy, or nut and cheese flavor, these recipes will satisfy your cravings and bring a smile to your face, as they are super healthy, guilt-free, and easy to make. Whether you are new to a plant-based diet, transitioning, or on it already, you can now enjoy raw, oil-free sweet potato chips, other vegetable or fruit chips, and raw cheese. Many of the recipes in this book call for using a dehydrator to make raw dishes. If you don't have a dehydrator, use the lowest setting on your oven. The dish won't be raw, but it will still be healthy. Just slice your favorite fruits—such as mangos, apples, pineapples, or bananas—or veggies, such as kale, zucchini, sweet potatoes, onion, or carrots. Sprinkle them with your favorite seasoning and dehydrate (or bake). Enjoy!

That's So Cheesy Vegan Macadamia Cheese

(raw/gluten-free)

Serves 2-4

2 cups macadamia nuts or cashews, soaked for 2 hours

1 teaspoon vegan probiotic

1 teaspoon dried onion flakes

1/3 teaspoon nutritional yeast

1/3 teaspoon salt

dried rosemary or thyme (optional)

TIP: When you make vegan cheese, raw or cooked, you can add agar agar, Irish moss, tapioca, or arrowroot flour if you want a denser, cheesier, and gooier texture. Just experiment with adding a little bit of each to the cheese recipes in this chapter.

DIRECTIONS:

1. Process soaked nuts in a high-speed blender with enough water to cover the nuts.

2. Using a nut milk bag, strain the mixture (save the strained milk for desserts, smoothies, or a coffee creamer).

3. Place the pulp and the remaining ingredients in a blender and mix until well combined.

4. Form mixture into a shape—you can use a stainless steel circle—and place on a Teflon sheet.

5. Dehydrate at 110°F for 12 hours or longer. Flip cheese over halfway through. You will get a crust on the outside, but the cheese will be soft inside. (The longer you dehydrate it, the crunchier it will be.)

6. Keep in a refrigerator for up to 5 days.

VARIATIONS: For the look of blue cheese, add a pinch of spirulina powder.

• To make fermented cheese, add 1/3 teaspoon salt, 1 teaspoon vegan probiotic, 1 teaspoon dried onion flakes, 1/3 teaspoon nutritional yeast, and spices of your choice.

• You can also use Brazil nuts or walnuts.

• If you don't have a dehydrator, you can still make this cheese, but it won't be raw. Use the lowest setting on the oven and bake it for about 45–60 minutes.

MACADAMIA NUT RICOTTA CHEESE (raw/gluten-free)

1 cup macadamia nuts
1 teaspoon vegan probiotic
pinch salt

DIRECTIONS:
1. Place macadamia nuts in a high-speed blender.
2. Cover the nuts with filtered water and mix well.
3. Add vegan probiotic and salt and gently stir.
4. Using a nut milk bag, strain the mixture (save the strained milk for desserts, smoothies, or a coffee creamer).
5. Use the pulp as a vegan ricotta cheese, perfect with **Not Corny but Creamy Corn Soup (see recipe page 125)**, over pasta, or with lasagna.

SEVENTH HEAVEN HAPPY COW CHEESE (raw/gluten-free)

2 cups raw cashews or macadamia nuts, soaked 4–6 hours and rinsed
juice of 1 lemon
2 garlic cloves
1/2 teaspoon garlic powder
2 tablespoons nutritional yeast
8 tablespoons water

DIRECTIONS:
1. Place all ingredients in a high-speed blender and blend until smooth. If you need, add a little bit more water so you can mix it well. You may have to stop and scrape the sides of the blender. Cheese is supposed to be smooth, but not too wet. If yours is too wet, use a nut bag to squeeze out the extra liquid.
2. Place the cheese mixture in a cheese mold or use parchment paper to wrap around. Let it sit in a refrigerator for a few hours to form.
3. Serve cheese in sandwiches, on crackers, with salads, or on a pizza. Cheese will stay fresh in a refrigerator for 5–7 days.

VARIATION: Add more salt or lemon juice, agar agar powder for thicker texture, or additional flavors inside or on top of the cheese, such as dill, rosemary, thyme, sun-dried tomatoes, parsley, red peppers, smoked paprika, curry powder, olives, wlanuts, etc. Sprinkle small pieces on top of the cheese and press in so they will set.

NUTTY PARMESAN POWDER CASHEW CHEESE (raw/gluten-free)

1 1/2 cups raw cashews (not soaked)
5–6 tablespoons nutritional yeast
1 teaspoon Celtic sea salt
1/2 teaspoon garlic powder, or more if you love garlic

DIRECTIONS:
1. Mix all ingredients in a high-speed blender or food processor until finely ground.
2. Store in a refrigerator in a glass container. The cheese will stay fresh for several weeks. Serve it over pizza, pasta, lasagna, salads, etc.

NOT YOUR MOM'S MOZZARELLA (gluten-free)

1 cup cashews, soaked
3/4 cup water
juice of 1/2 lemon
3 tablespoons nutritional yeast
1/2 teaspoon garlic powder
1/2 teaspoon pink Himalayan salt
4 tablespoons tapioca flour

DIRECTIONS:
1. Blend all ingredients except tapioca flour in a high-speed blender.
2. Transfer mixture to a small pot. Add tapioca flour and mix.
3. Cook on very low heat while stirring for about 10 minutes or until thickened. Be careful not to burn the cheese. The mixture should be thick and gooey and not come off a spoon.
4. Fold into a mold or scoop out with an ice cream scoop to form mozzarella balls.
5. Store in a refrigerator for a few days or freeze for later.

VARIATIONS: If you want the cheese gooier, add less tapioca flour. If you want it firmer, add more.
• Add fresh herbs or turmeric for a different flavor.

This Pesto Is the Besto!

by Stefany and Gianna Oliva
(inspired by Italian heritage)
(raw/gluten-free)

Stefany Oliva is Gianna's mom. She worked as a teacher's assistant with Aleksandra Winters. Gianna was an art student of Mrs. Winters. They are happy to share their favorite Italian recipe enjoyed by their family for over ten years.

Serves 1
3 cups fresh basil leaves
1 cup pine nuts
1 cup walnuts
4 cloves garlic
1/4 cup nutritional yeast
3/4 cup olive oil
1 teaspoon salt
pepper to taste

DIRECTIONS:
1. In a food processor, blend basil leaves, pine nuts, walnuts, garlic, and yeast.
2. Slowly pour in oil while pulsing. Stir in salt and pepper to taste. Enjoy over pasta with **Go Nuts for Pine Nuts Parmesan Cheese** (recipe follows).

TIP: Use ice-cube trays or small containers to freeze leftover pesto for later.

GO NUTS FOR PINE NUTS PARMESAN CHEESE
(raw/gluten-free)

2 cups raw pine nuts
3–4 tablespoons nutritional yeast
1/2 teaspoon Celtic sea salt
1–2 tablespoons fresh lemon juice
2 cloves garlic
1 cup water

DIRECTIONS:
1. Mix all ingredients in a high-speed blender or food processor until finely ground. If you need, add more water. Use a spatula to spread a thin layer of the mixture onto Teflon sheets.
2. Dehydrate at 110 °F for 8-10 hours or longer until dry. Flip over halfway through. You should get a crunchy texture, like Parmesan cheese. When texture is right, break into small pieces. Dehydrate longer until you achieve desired texture.
3. Keep in a refrigerator in a glass jar for up to 4-5 weeks or freeze for several months. Serve it over pizza, pasta, lasagna, salads, etc. It tastes great with pesto sauce and pasta.

VARIATION: Add 2-3 tablespoons of dry red wine to the mixture for a gourmet taste.

CASHEW SOUR CREAM
(raw/gluten-free)

1 cup raw cashews
3/4 cup water
1/4 teaspoon pink Himalayan salt
pinch black pepper
pinch chili pepper
1/3 teaspoon nutritional yeast
1 tablespoon lemon juice

DIRECTIONS: Mix all ingredients in a high-speed blender.

LIMA BEAN DIP (gluten-free)

Serves 8

4 cups cooked lima beans
1/2 cup sun-dried tomatoes
4 cloves garlic
juice from 1/2 lemon or more
1 teaspoon nutritional yeast
1/2 teaspoon onion powder
1/2 teaspoon salt
1/8 teaspoon paprika, or more to taste
pinch black pepper

DIRECTIONS:

1. Place all ingredients in a food processor and blend until smooth.

VARIATION: Experiment with different kinds of beans and lentils.

CREAMY VEGAN MAYO
(raw/gluten-free)

1 cup cashews or macadamia nuts
1/2 cup water
2 tablespoons lemon juice or apple cider vinegar
1 tablespoon mustard
1 tablespoon nutritional yeast
1/4 teaspoon sea salt
2 drops Natural Liquid Smoke (hickory smoke) by Living Nutritionals
pinch cayenne pepper

DIRECTIONS:

1. Blend all ingredients in a high-speed blender until smooth.
2. Serve with your favorite dishes, such as **The Burger She Wrote (see recipe page 169)**.

IT'S RAINING KETCHUP HALLELUJAH
(raw/gluten-free)

1 cup sun-dried tomatoes, soaked in filtered water for 20 minutes
2 tablespoons goji berries, soaked in filtered water for 20 minutes
1 medium-sized tomato, chopped
4 Medjool dates
1 clove garlic
2 tablespoons lemon juice
3 tablespoons raw macadamia nuts or cashews
1/2 teaspoon Celtic sea salt
pinch black pepper

DIRECTIONS:

1. Drain tomatoes and goji berries, reserving some of the tomato soaking water.
2. In a high-speed blender, mix tomatoes, berries, and all remaining ingredients. Slowly add some of the reserved tomato water, mixing until you achieve your desired consistency. You want the ketchup to be thick, not watery, so don't add too much water.
3. Store in a refrigerator for up to a few days.

HAPPY PIGS COCONUT BACON
(raw/gluten-free)

2 cups coconut flakes (not shredded coconut)
4–5 tablespoons coconut aminos or liquid aminos
1 tablespoon maple syrup
a few drops Natural Liquid Smoke (hickory smoke) by Living Nutritionals for BBQ flavor or 1 teaspoon BBQ sauce

DIRECTIONS:

1. Mix all ingredients until well incorporated. For raw "bacon," dehydrate at 110–115°F for about 4–8 hours until crunchy, depending on humidity. For baked, use an oven and bake at 250°F until crispy, 15–20 minutes.
2. Store in a glass jar for up to a few weeks. Use in salads, soups, stews, or desserts. So good!

NACH YO BUSINESS NACHOS
(gluten-free)

Serves 6-8

8 cups organic tortilla chips, restaurant style
2 cups beans, cooked
Seventh Heaven Happy Cow Cheese
(see recipe page 87)

TOPPINGS:

Cashew Sour Cream (see recipe page 90),
I Feel Saucy (see recipe page 97),
chopped cilantro, halved cherry tomatoes,
sliced pickles, chopped onions, chopped bell pepper,
sliced jalapeño, corn, salsa, sliced avocado.

DIRECTIONS

1. Preheat oven to 350°F.

2. Combine tortilla chips, beans, and cheese in a deep baking dish. Bake for 10–15 minutes.

3. Take out of oven and carefully transfer to a big plate (be careful, as the items will be hot).

4. Garnish with your choice of toppings.

VARIATION: Try these yummy vegan nachos with **Cowgirl Southwestern Bean Salad (see recipe page 115).**

CRUNCHY ROSEMARY CRACKERS
(gluten-free)

Serves 20-24

Dry ingredients:
1 cup almond flour
1 cup millet flour
1 tablespoon nutritional yeast
1 teaspoon salt
1/2 teaspoon aluminum-free baking powder
1/2 teaspoon curry powder
pinch paprika
1 bunch fresh rosemary for flavor
Wet ingredients:
1/2 cup flaxseed meal/ flour
1/2 cup water
1 tablespoon olive oil or melted coconut oil

DIRECTIONS:

1. Preheat oven to 350°F.

2. In a large bowl, mix dry ingredients first, and then add wet ingredients.

3. Mix well and spread mixture on parchment paper on a large cookie sheet. Use a spatula to pat it evenly and thinly. Cut into squares for approximately 24 crackers.

4. Bake for 30 minutes. Flip crackers over and bake for additional 15 minutes or until ready. Serve warm or store for later.

5. Use with **Seventh Heaven Happy Cow Cheese (see recipe page 87), Friends and Family Hummus (see recipe page 102),** salads, or soups.

VARIATIONS: Sprinkle on additional toppings before baking, such as sesame seeds, pumpkin or sunflower seeds, chia seeds, flax seeds, hemp seeds, crushed walnuts, cranberries, olives, or sun-dried tomatoes.
 • Drizzle on some lemon juice, add fresh or dried herbs, or use spices, such as garlic powder, onion powder, or pepper flakes, etc.

BBQ Jackfruit

(gluten-free)

Serves 6-8

1 can green jackfruit, drained
1 cup your favorite BBQ sauce
1 small yellow onion, sliced thinly
1 cup maitake or oyster mushrooms, chopped
1/2 cup water
2-3 cloves of garlic

DIRECTIONS:

1. In a small pot or skillet, combine jackfruit with BBQ sauce. Let marinate for at least 1 hour.
2. When ready, heat it up over medium heat. Add onions, garlic, mushrooms, and water. Reduce heat and sauté until caramelized, about 10 - 20 minutes. Add additional spices if you want. Set aside.
3. Serve over nachos, tacos, or on a sandwich.

VARIATION: For a more intense smoky flavor, add a few drops of chicory liquid smoke after it has been cooked.

BBQ Tofu

(gluten-free)

Serves 6-8

1 package organic, non-GMO, firm or sprouted tofu
1/2 cup water
1/2 cup favorite BBQ sauce

DIRECTIONS:

1. Preheat oven to 400°F.
2. Slice tofu and place in a glass or ceramic pot with water and BBQ sauce, making sure that the tofu is evenly coated with the sauce.
3. Reduce the heat to 350°F and place the tofu in the oven. Bake for 20-30 minutes.
4. Serve over a salad, quinoa, or rice.

VARIATION: Add veggies and avocado to make your favorite sandwich or a wrap.

Potato Pancakes
Placki Ziemniaczane

by Tadeusz Gruba (Poland)

Tadeusz Gruba is my stepfather. He works as a manager at a facility that freezes fruits and vegetables. Tadeusz lives in a small town in Poland called Sobieszyn. He has a big garden where he grows a variety of organic fruits, vegetables, and herbs. Tadeusz is passionate about natural farming, composting, and horticulture. In his free time, he tends to his garden, cooks, and plays an accordion to entertain his family and friends. This is a traditional Polish dish. It is fried, but so good! You can serve these pancakes with mushroom sauce, mustard, applesauce, or **Cashew Sour Cream** (see recipe page 90).

Serves 2-4 (gluten-free)
2 pounds white potatoes (don't use baby potatoes)
1 small onion
2 flax eggs (see Egg Substitutes For Baking page 47)
1 tablespoon white flour
1/2 teaspoon salt or to taste
black pepper to taste
coconut oil, for frying

DIRECTIONS:
1. Peel potatoes and grate on the fine side of a grater. Then, grate the onion. Place both in a mixing bowl.
2. Add flax eggs, flour, salt, and pepper to bowl and mix.
3. Heat coconut oil in a frying pan. Form small pancakes from the potato mixture and fry. When the pancakes become golden, flip them over and fry the other side.
4. Serve immediately with your favorite sauce.

VARIATION: If you prefer baked pancakes, preheat the oven to 400°F. Place pancakes on a greased, flat baking sheet. Bake for 25 minutes or until golden.

FLOURLESS BREAD
(gluten-free)

Serves 8-10
3/4 cup flax seeds
1 cup sunflower seeds
1 1/2 cups gluten-free oats
1/2 cup almonds
10 tablespoons flaxseed meal
5 tablespoons coconut oil, melted
1 tablespoon maple syrup
2 teaspoons salt

DIRECTIONS:
1. In a big bowl, combine 1 cup warm water with the flax seeds. Let it sit for about 30 minutes, until sticky.
2. Add remaining ingredients and mix gently by hand. You may experiment with other ingredients and add sun-dried tomatoes, sun-dried olives, fresh herbs, cranberries, prunes, or nuts.
3. Grease a loaf pan and fold in the dough. Bake in a preheated oven to 300°F for 45-60 minutes, or until ready.
4. Let cool and then wait about 12 hours until you slice it. Otherwise, it will fall apart.

VARIATION: You can also process all the ingredients in a food processor and bake the bread flat on a big cookie sheet. Then cut into crackers if you prefer.

HAPPY CHICKEN BBQ CAULIFLOWER WINGS
(gluten-free)

Serves 2-4
1 medium cauliflower
1 cup natural BBQ sauce of your choice
1/2 cup unsweetened nut milk (almond, cashew, or coconut)
2 tablespoons liquid aminos or coconut aminos
2 tablespoons coconut flour or almond flour (meal)
1 tablespoon nutritional yeast
1 teaspoon apple cider vinegar
1 teaspoon garlic or onion powder
1 teaspoon paprika (I used smoked)

1/2 teaspoon curry powder
1/8 teaspoon cayenne pepper
2–3 drops Natural Liquid Smoke by Living Nutritionals for stronger flavor (optional)
salt, to taste
pinch ground pepper

DIRECTIONS:
1. Preheat oven to 450°F. Line a cookie sheet with parchment paper.
2. Wash cauliflower and break into bite-sized florets.
3. Mix all remaining ingredients together in a large bowl or a high-speed blender to create a batter.
4. Dip a cauliflower floret into batter and ensure it is evenly coated. Place on cookie sheet and repeat until all the florets are coated.
5. Bake for 15 minutes or until golden brown. Then flip florets around and bake for additional 5-10 minutes until ready.
6. Serve with celery sticks and **I Feel Saucy (recipe follows)**.

I FEEL SAUCY
(raw/gluten-free)

1 1/2 cups cashews or macadamia nuts
1 1/2 cups water (less if you want thicker sauce)
2–3 cloves garlic
4–5 tablespoons apple cider vinegar
3–4 tablespoons lemon juice
3 teaspoons onion powder
1 teaspoon dried dill or 2 tablespoons fresh, chopped dill
1 teaspoon garlic powder
1/2 teaspoon paprika
1 teaspoon pink Himalayan salt
pinch black pepper

DIRECTIONS:
1. In a high-speed blender, process all ingredients until smooth.
2. Store in a glass container, refrigerated, for 3–5 days.
3. Use as a dipping sauce or a salad dressing.

Friends and Family Hummus
by Arnon Kedem (Israel)

Arnon Kedem was born in Israel, where hummus is plentiful. Falafel and hummus are as popular as pizza and hamburgers are in America. After living in the United States for more than thirty years and eating commercially made hummus, he decided to venture into the kitchen and try making his own. It took about one year of attempts to perfect his recipe. He makes a large amount to share with friends and family.

Serves 2-4 (gluten-free)
1 pound dried chickpeas
1 tablespoon baking soda
5–8 garlic cloves
juice of 2 lemons
1 cup tahini sauce
1/4 cup olive oil or water
3 tablespoons red sriracha sauce or 1 1/2 tablespoons harissa (optional)
1 tablespoon salt

DIRECTIONS:
1. Wash and soak chickpeas overnight with enough water for boiling in a pot.
2. Boil chickpeas with baking soda for about 1 hour or until soft. Scoop out foam while boiling (do not mix it in).
3. Strain water out, reserving one glass of water, and let the chickpeas cool in the fridge.
4. Place all ingredients except chickpeas and reserved water in a food processor and mix for 3–4 minutes. Add chickpeas and slowly pour in the reserved water to get the consistency you like.
5. Let cool before serving.

VARIATION: You can serve the hummus with olive oil on top, and with any of the following garnishes: parsley, paprika, pine nuts, or chopped dried tomatoes.

Olenko's Mom's Bread

Anna Gruba is my mom. She is a retired lawyer and lives in Poland. Anna has a beautiful garden in a small town called Sobieszyn where she grows a variety of organic fruit, vegetables, and herbs. She loves cooking and baking. When she is not in the kitchen, you can find her playing with her grandson Kubuś; picking fruit and vegetables in the garden; or picking mushrooms in the nearby forest. Anna's home is nestled in a beautiful, natural surrounding.

Serves 12-14

2 tablespoons warm water (not hot)

1 teaspoon coconut sugar

1 pack active dry yeast, non-GMO

6 cups all-purpose flour (I used King Arthur 100 percent organic bread flour)

2 teaspoons salt (Real Salt or sea salt)

4 cups warm water (if too thick, add more water)

1 cup pumpkin seeds

1 cup walnuts

8 tablespoons oatmeal

1 tablespoon flax seeds

1 tablespoon chia seeds

VARIATIONS: Try this recipe with half rye flour and half barley.
• For a gluten-free version, use half rice and half millet.
• Use various molds to make rolls, baguettes, or bagels. They will bake faster than the bread.
• Set aside 1/2 cup plain dough (without seeds or oatmeal) and use it as a "starter" in place of active dry yeast next time you make the bread. Store in a glass container in a refrigerator for 1-2 weeks.

DIRECTIONS:

1. Mix warm water, coconut sugar, and yeast gently and cover with a cloth. Set aside in a warm place to rise for 30 minutes.

2. Once the yeast has risen, gently mix flour, salt, and warm water in a big glass or ceramic bowl. Add the yeast mixture. Knead gently with your hands until the lumps disappear, or use a bread-making machine. Cover with a cloth and set aside to allow to rise until doubled, 2–4 hours. Keep in a warm place. The warmer the room temperature, the faster it will rise.

3. Once the dough has risen, add the pumpkin seeds, walnuts, oatmeal, and flax seeds. Mix gently with your hands. Set aside for about 30 minutes to rise.

4. Preheat oven to 360°F. Grease and flour a loaf pan. You can use one long, narrow pan or two smaller bread pans.

5. Place dough in loaf pan. Sprinkle chia seeds on top. Place in the oven and raise the temperature to 410°F. Bake for 70 minutes or longer depending on the size of your loaf pan.

Cmac N Roll

by Elizabeth Aprile
(inspired by her love of Latin culture)
(raw/gluten-free)

Elizabeth Aprile is a hard-working single mother of four who is always searching for quick, tasty, and healthy meals to prepare for her family. Her busy schedule of work, dance, fitness, chauffeuring, and helping with homework allows for little time to be creative in the kitchen. Aleksandra's first cookbook, *Raw Food Art: Four Seasons of Plant-Powered Goodness*, introduced Elizabeth to quick and easy ways to work with fresh, wholesome ingredients in their purest form, resulting in meals her entire family enjoys. Thanks to Olenko, Elizabeth now takes greater care of what she puts on the table and in the mouths of her family.

3 very ripe Hass avocados (soft to the touch, but not mushy)
2 vine-ripened tomatoes, seeded and diced
juice of 2 limes
1/2 red onion, diced
1 bunch cilantro, removed from stems and finely chopped
2 cloves garlic, crushed
1 teaspoon kosher salt

DIRECTIONS:
1. Halve and pit avocados. Remove from skin and spoon into a mixing bowl. Mash with a fork, keeping the avocado just a little bit chunky.
2. Add remaining ingredients and mix well.
3. Place in a bowl and serve with **Nach Yo Business Nachos (see recipe page 93).**

Pick Me Up Polish Pickles

by Tadeusz Szewczyk (Poland)
(raw/gluten-free)

Tadeusz Szewczyk lives with his family in Poland. He and his wife, Dorota, own a beautiful organic orchard and a garden where they grow a wide variety of fruits, vegetables, flowers, and herbs. He loves cooking and incorporating fresh ingredients into his dishes. Tadeusz is famous for this pickle recipe among his family and friends.

1 tablespoon coarse salt
5 dry dill flowers
2–3 fresh horseradish leaves
2–3 oak or currant leaves (optional)
Kirby cucumbers
2 teaspoons mustard seeds
4-5 bay leaves
a few grains allspice
5 cloves garlic (or more)
3 inches horseradish root

DIRECTIONS:
1. Make the brine: In a pot, bring 1 liter water to a boil and add salt.
2. Arrange 4 dill flowers and horseradish leaves on the bottom of a stoneware or glass dish along with oak or currant leaves if you wish.
3. Wash cucumbers. Remove blossom ends and make a crosswise 1/3-inch-deep cut. Place cucumbers in the dish cut-side up.
4. Add spices, garlic, and horseradish root to dish with cucumbers. Cover with a dill flower and pour in the brine, which should be at room temperature. Make sure the brine covers the cucumbers and the dill. You may place a small plate on top to keep pressure on the cucumbers.
5. Your pickles will be ready after 24 hours and should be consumed within 2–3 days.

CHAPTER 11

What's So Spicy About Spices and Fresh About Herbs?

Spices, herbs, and essential oils have been used for ages in many countries and cultures as natural remedies, food flavorings, insect repellent, and even protection from evil spirits. They smell and taste good, and they uplift our mood. They can be used in cooking, folk medicine, and body care. They can also be mixed with other natural ingredients to make natural cleaning products. They are very powerful and effective. If you are interested in learning more about them, visit your local naturalistic doctor, herbal store, or any medical professional who is experienced in natural remedies.

HERBS

Herbs are important in every cuisine, but I think they are critical in a vegan, plant-based diet because they can help transform ordinary fruits and vegetables into spectacular and mouthwatering dishes. They come in many forms: fresh, dried, freeze-dried, ground, in single formulas, or in spice-herb mixes. You can chop fresh herbs and freeze them to have them handy in the winter. The following are some of the most popular herbs:

• basil	• bay leaves	• chives	• cilantro
• lavender	• lemon balm	• oregano	• parsley
• peppermint	• rosemary	• sage	• tarragon
• thyme	• dill	• coriander	• fennel

You can grow your own organic herbs all year round. I plant herbs in big pots on my deck in the springtime. I transfer them to small pots and bring many of them inside in the fall, so I can enjoy fresh herbs in the winter season. My family has a huge organic garden in Poland, and they grow so many herbs. Some even grow wild.

Olenko's Favorite Super Plants

Here are a few natural plant suggestions to help you thrive. You can drink them as a tea or tincture, or use them in smoothies and salads:

• cilantro	• dandelion	• garlic	• ginger
• holy basil	• milk thistle	• moringa	• onion
• parsley	• red clover	• spirulina	• stinging nettle
• turmeric	• bay laurel	• ashwaganda	• ginseng

Contact an herbalist or naturopathic doctor for a detox program or natural folk remedies.

SPICES

Spices can come as powders or as a whole dried plant that you can grind. Use a clean coffee grinder to grind whole seeds into a powder. You can roast, cook, and bake with spices; make powerful elixirs; add them to smoothies and juices; and even use them to make a body cream, toothpaste, or face mask.

Toasting spices is one of several ways of coaxing flavors out of them. What is special about toasted spices is the way the dry heat transforms them, both drawing out their aromas and adding a mellow, toasty complexity. Visit your local health-food store or an ethnic supermarket to smell and try unique new spices.

Every culture has its distinctive spice mix that is used for specific dishes. Experiment and have fun with them in your kitchen. The following are the most popular spices:

• allspice	• anise	• black pepper	• turmeric
• cardamom	• cumin	• cayenne pepper	• garlic
• chili powder	• cloves	• curry	• paprika
• ginger	• onion	• oregano	• sesame seeds
• saffron	• white pepper	• vanilla	• cinnamon

ESSENTIAL OILS

Essential oils have been used for thousands of years, ever since ancient and biblical times. There are so many kinds of oils to choose from. The company I love and trust is Young Living. Their oils are one hundred percent pure and therapeutic. Their Vitality line has been FDA approved for internal consumption and cooking.

Many of the therapeutic-grade essential oils—such as lavender, peppermint, lemon, or lime—are great for flavoring desserts and savory dishes. Be sure to always check the source of the essential oil that you take internally, and be careful if you are pregnant or nursing.

EDIBLE FLOWERS

Flowers are perfect if you want to create edible food art. You can see many recipes in my first cookbook, *Raw Food Art: Four Seasons of Plant-Based Goodness.* You can use edible flowers to decorate your desserts, such as cakes and smoothies, or use them in sandwiches or salads. There are many flowers that are edible. Refer to books about edible plants and flowers.

Eat flowers you have grown by yourself or know to be safe for consumption. Don't eat flowers from the florist or nursery because they have probably been sprayed with pesticides or other chemicals. Many farmers' markets sell edible flowers. Always check to be sure that the flowers are safe to eat. If you are unsure, don't consume them. If you have any food allergies or seasonal allergies, ask your medical practitioner if it is safe for you to consume edible flowers.

The following are a few edible flowers and blossoms you may grow yourself:

- angelica
- basil
- carnation
- chive blossom
- clover
- dandelion
- lavender
- marigold
- nasturtium
- pansy
- rose
- snap dragon
- sunflower
- violet
- zucchini
- borage

Contact an herbalist or naturopathic doctor for a detox program or natural folk remedies.

OLD ALL SPICE POLISH FOREST MIX

2 tablespoons marjoram
2 tablespoons onion powder or dried minced onion
2 tablespoons garlic powder or garlic salt
1 tablespoon black pepper
1 tablespoon juniper berries
1 teaspoon caraway seeds
1/2 teaspoon allspice (ground or whole berry)
1/4 teaspoon ground bay leaf

DIRECTIONS:

1. Grind all spices in a high-speed blender or a coffee grinder.
2. Store in an airtight container at room temperature. Use with sauces, salads, soups, or stews.

Olenko's Kitchen Revolution Toasted Cumin Spice Mix

This spice mix is great for salads, soups, sauces, dressings, stews, or sandwiches. When you make it, the whole house will smell amazing.

4 tablespoons cumin seeds
1/4 cup walnuts
1/4 cup pumpkin seeds
1 tablespoon brown flax seeds
2 tablespoons nutritional yeast
1 teaspoon turmeric powder
1/3 teaspoon pink Himalayan salt
1/2 teaspoon onion powder
1/4 teaspoon cayenne pepper

DIRECTIONS:

1. Place cumin seeds in a small skillet over medium-low heat and shake the pan occasionally to prevent burning. The cumin seeds will be toasted when you can smell their aroma.
2. Transfer cumin seeds immediately to a spice grinder or high-speed blender and process into powder. Transfer the powder to a glass container.
3. In a high-speed blender, process walnuts, pumpkin seeds, and flax seeds into a powder. (Be careful not to overprocess; if you do, you will get nut butter.) Add this powder to the cumin, and then add remaining ingredients.
4. Mix well. Store in a glass container in the refrigerator of freezer for several weeks.

VARIATIONS: Experiment with adding other spices, such as paprika, ginger, cinnamon, garlic powder, chili peppers, rosemary, oregano, dried basil, parsley, dill, and thyme.

RAS EL HANOUT MOROCCAN SPICE

1 teaspoon ground cumin
1 teaspoon ground ginger
1 teaspoon salt
3/4 teaspoon freshly ground black pepper
1/2 teaspoon ground cinnamon
1/2 teaspoon ground coriander seeds
1/2 teaspoon cayenne pepper
1/2 teaspoon ground allspice
1/4 teaspoon ground cloves

DIRECTIONS: Combine all spices and store in an airtight container at room temperature.

TOASTED CURRY SPICE

2 tablespoons whole cumin seeds, toasted
2 tablespoons whole cardamom seeds, toasted
2 tablespoons whole coriander seeds, toasted
1/4 cup ground turmeric
1 tablespoon dry mustard
1 teaspoon cayenne pepper

DIRECTIONS: Grind all whole seeds. Combine all spices and store in an airtight container at room temperature.

JAMAICAN CURRY SPICE

1/4 cup whole coriander seeds
2 tablespoons whole cumin seeds
2 tablespoons whole mustard seeds
2 tablespoons whole anise seeds
1 tablespoon whole fenugreek seeds
1 tablespoon whole allspice berries
5 tablespoons ground turmeric

DIRECTIONS: Grind all whole seeds. Combine all spices and store in an airtight container at room temperature. Use with soups, stews, sauces, salads, dips, etc.

PUMPKIN SPICE

1 teaspoon ground cinnamon
1/4 teaspoon ground nutmeg
1/4 teaspoon ground ginger
1/8 teaspoon ground cloves
1/4 teaspoon vanilla powder (optional)

DIRECTIONS: Combine all ingredients and store in an airtight container at room temperature. Use for baking, desserts, hot cacao, coffee, etc.

ZA'ATAR SPICE

1 tablespoon fresh oregano, chopped
1 tablespoon sumac (you can find it at Middle Eastern markets)
1 1/2 tablespoons ground cumin
1 tablespoon sesame seeds
1 teaspoon kosher salt
1 teaspoon freshly ground black pepper

DIRECTIONS: Combine herbs and store in an airtight container at room temperature. Use with salads, soups, stews, crackers, etc. Mixture will stay fresh for about 2 weeks.

HERBES DE PROVENCE

2 tablespoons dried rosemary
2 tablespoons dried savory
2 tablespoons dried thyme
2 tablespoons dried basil
2 tablespoons dried marjoram
2 tablespoons dried lavender flowers
2 tablespoons dried Italian parsley
1 tablespoon fennel seed
1 tablespoon dried oregano
1 tablespoon dried tarragon
1 teaspoon bay powder

DIRECTIONS: Combine herbs and store in an airtight container at room temperature. Use with cheese, dips, salads, potatoes, pasta, soups, and savory dishes.

CHAPTER 12

It's Lunchtime: Salad or Soup a Day Keeps the Doctor Away!

I love, love, love salads. I could exist on a salad diet only. You can eat salads as a side dish or an appetizer. Enjoy them from a mung bowl with many other grains, over raw zucchini noodles, or on a cabbage leaf. As another alternative, use a rice-paper wrap, coconut wrap, lettuce leaf, collard greens leaf, or kale leaf for a healthy, delicious lunch.

TUTTI FRUTTI ARUGULA SALAD
(raw/gluten-free)

Serves 2-4
6 cups baby arugula or spinach
1 cup dark grapes, halved
1 cup strawberries, sliced
1 cup almonds
1 purple onion, chopped
6–8 fresh figs, halved
balsamic vinegar
That's So Cheesy Vegan Macadamia Cheese (see recipe page 86)

DIRECTIONS:
1. In a big bowl, toss arugula, grapes, strawberries, almonds, and onion. Arrange figs on top.
2. Dress with balsamic vinegar and serve with **Nut Cheese (see recipes Chapter 10)** or **Happy Pigs Coconut Bacon (see recipe page 92).**

VARIATIONS: Use any fruit that is in season, such as raspberries, watermelon, blueberries, persimmon, pomegranate, peaches, pears, or apples.
   • Try the salad with different nuts—such as walnuts, pecans, and hazelnuts—or raisins.

SAVE THE TUNA SALAD
(gluten-free)

Serves 4–6
3 cups cooked chickpeas
1 cup pecans, chopped
1/2 cup celery, chopped
2 1/2 tablespoons purple onion, chopped
2 tablespoons mustard
2 tablespoons apple cider vinegar
1 teaspoon or more of chopped fresh herbs: basil, parsley, dill, etc.
1 teaspoon Celtic salt or pink Himalayan salt
1/4 teaspoon black pepper
pinch of cayenne pepper

DIRECTIONS: Place all ingredients in a big bowl and gently mix together.

VARIATIONS: Add avocado or tahini if you prefer a creamier taste.
   • Serve with **Olenko's Mom's Bread (see recipe page 98)**, rolls, or as a wrap.

POLISH SLAW
(raw/gluten-free)

Serves 4–6
1 medium-head cabbage, shredded
2 carrots, chopped
1 onion, chopped
1 apple, grated (peel first if not organic)
handful of cilantro or parsley, chopped
lemon juice to taste
apple cider vinegar to taste
salt to taste
pepper to taste
1/2 cup **Cashew Sour Cream (see recipe page 90)**

DIRECTIONS:
1. Mix together all ingredients except the cashew cream.
2. Add the cream and mix again.

VARIATION: Add raisins.

POLISH VEGETABLE SALAD
(gluten-free)

Serves 2-4
5 carrots
5 parsnips
1 celeriac
3 potatoes
16 ounces corn (cooked or frozen)
16 ounces peas (cooked or frozen)
2–3 pickles or more to your taste
2 apples
1 onion
3–4 tablespoons mustard
juice of 1 lemon
dill, parsley, or cilantro (optional)
Cashew Sour Cream (see recipe page 90)

DIRECTIONS:
1. Wash and cook carrots, parsnips, celeriac, and potatoes. You may cook them with the skin on and peel afterward (cooked vegetables peel very easily).
2. Cube all the vegetables. Place in a big bowl and mix together with the mustard and lemon juice.
3. Fold the cashew cream over the vegetables in the bowl and gently mix.

UNICORN'S DELIGHT VEGGIE RAINBOW SALAD
(raw/gluten-free)

This salad tastes great with **The Burger She Wrote (see recipe page 169)**.

Serves 2-4
Salad:
1 head of lettuce, chopped
1 cup thinly shredded purple cabbage
5 radishes, chopped
2 tomatoes, chopped
2 avocados, chopped
1 red bell pepper, chopped
1 green bell pepper, chopped
1 small onion, chopped
1 cucumber, chopped
olives, chopped (optional)
handful of cilantro, chopped
Dressing:
juice of 1/2 lemon
4–5 tablespoons apple cider vinegar
1 tablespoon **Go Nuts for Pine Nuts Parmesan Cheese (see recipe page 90)**

DIRECTIONS:
1. In a big bowl, combine all salad ingredients.
2. Prepare the dressing in a separate dish.
3. Add the dressing to the salad and mix gently.

POLISH LEEK SALAD
(raw/gluten-free)

Serves 2-4
2 leeks, washed thoroughly in between the leaves and cut into thin strips
1 apple, shredded
2 carrots, shredded
2–3 tablespoons lemon juice
pepper to taste
1/2 cup **Cashew Sour Cream (see recipe page 90)**

DIRECTIONS: In a large bowl, combine all ingredients and toss to coat with cream.

COUNT YOUR BLESSINGS
LENTIL SALAD (gluten-free)
Serves 8

1 pound lentils, cooked
1 small onion, chopped
1 cucumber, cubed
1 avocado, cubed
1 cup cherry tomatoes, cut into halves
1 bunch parsley, chopped
1 clove garlic, chopped
2 tablespoons olive oil
juice of 1/2 lemon
salt to taste

DIRECTIONS: Combine all ingredients in a big bowl and mix until well incorporated.

EAT THE RAINBOW FRUIT SALAD
by Kubuś Grabarczyk (Poland)

This salad can be made by children. My nephew Kubuś Grabarczyk loves to make it. He is six years old and lives in Poland with my younger sister, Gosia, and her husband, Tomek. Kubuś loves to play in his grandmother's magical garden by the forest. He likes nature, mushroom picking, fruits, vegetables, painting, dinosaurs, and squirrels. He plays soccer in his free time.

Serves 1-2 (raw/gluten-free)
4 mandarins, sliced
2 kiwis, sliced
1 cup pineapple, cubed
1 banana, sliced
1 pear, sliced
1 apple, sliced
1 bunch of purple grapes
1/2 cup blueberries
1/2 cup raspberries
1/2 cup blackberries

DIRECTIONS: Place all ingredients in a bowl and mix or create rainbow skewers.

VARIATION: Add dried cranberries, pineapple, or raisins instead of grapes.

CHICKPEA AND BEET WILL MAKE YOU STRONG AND SWEET
by Lidia Bis (Poland)

Lidia Bis was born in Poland but resides in the United States. She is a high school teacher and an avid promoter of healthy living. Her transition to a healthy lifestyle began several years ago when she decided to use food as her medicine. She stopped eating meat mainly for ethical reasons after watching a documentary called Earthlings. She became a vegan shortly after.

She has been enjoying the plant-based diet and encourages others to eat healthier. Her passion for mindful living includes activities that bring joy to her soul, such as spending time in nature, using natural skin care and essential oils, meditating, listening to soothing music, dancing, traveling, appreciating all living beings, and much more. Lidia has been a close friend of Aleksandra's for as long as both have lived in the United States. Aleksandra's expertise influenced Lidia's culinary choices and eating habits.

Serves 4–6 (gluten-free)
3 large red beets
1/2 onion
1/2 bunch cilantro
14 ounces firm tofu
1 1/2 cups chickpeas, cooked
juice of 1 lemon
2 tablespoons olive oil
salt to taste
pepper to taste

DIRECTIONS:
1. Cook beets in water until soft. Don't overcook; you want them to be a little firm. Drain the water and set beets aside to cool.
2. Chop onion and cilantro, and crumble tofu. Place in a bowl. Add chickpeas.
3. Peel beets and cut into cubes. Add to bowl.
4. In a separate dish, prepare the dressing by mixing the lemon juice and olive oil. Pour over vegetables in bowl. Season with salt and pepper to taste.

CREAMY DILL CUCUMBER SALAD
(raw/gluten-free)

This side dish, also by Lidia Bis, is popular on a hot summer day, usually served with roasted potatoes.

Serves 2–4
2 long organic cucumbers
1/4 teaspoon salt
pepper to taste
non-dairy yogurt or plain **Cashew Sour Cream (see recipe page 90)**
2 tablespoons apple cider vinegar
juice of 1/2 lemon
2 tablespoons sweetener of choice (agave, maple syrup, coconut nectar)
2 tablespoons fresh dill, chopped

DIRECTIONS:
1. If the cucumbers are organic, you may leave the skin on; if nonorganic, peel first. Use the mandoline side of a grater to slice the cucumbers. If you don't have a grater, use a knife to slice them thinly.
2. Place cucumber in a mixing bowl. Add salt and pepper and mix well. Set aside for a few minutes (the salt will make the cucumber softer).
3. In a separate dish, mix yogurt, vinegar, lemon juice, and sweetener. Fold yogurt mixture into the bowl with the cucumber and mix well.
4. Add fresh dill and serve.

Forbidden Salad

According to legend, the name "forbidden rice" dates from ancient China, when only the emperor was allowed to eat this grain. It was forbidden for everyone else. It is made of heirloom/purple/black rice and has a nutty taste. It is one of the most nutritious ancient grains. It contains many antioxidants and nutrients.

Serves 8-10 (gluten-free)
3 cups purple forbidden rice, cooked
3 cups lentils, cooked
2 cups lima beans, cooked
2 peppers, chopped
2 avocados, cubed
1 cup organic corn
1 cucumber, cubed
1 small red onion, chopped
1/2 cup baby tomatoes
1/2 cup pumpkin seeds
1/2 cup sunflower seeds
3 tablespoons apple cider vinegar (adjust to your taste)
curry powder, to taste
fresh herbs: basil, mint, parsley, cilantro
salt
pepper

DIRECTIONS: Combine all ingredients in a big bowl. Mix gently until well incorporated.

ZA'ATAR CHICKPEA SALAD
(gluten-free)

Serves 4
Salad:
2 cups cooked chickpeas
1–2 tablespoons **Za'atar Spice (see recipe page 106)**
1 tablespoon raw apple cider vinegar
1 tablespoon hemp-seed oil or good quality olive oil
juice of 1/2 lemon
2 tablespoons raw tahini
1/2 teaspoon salt
1/3 teaspoon cumin
pinch of cayenne pepper
4 cups baby spinach
1 small purple onion, chopped
1 avocado, cubed
3 tablespoons sunflower seeds
fresh lemon juice (optional)
Toppings:
sweet pea shoots
edible flowers
fresh parsley
cilantro

DIRECTIONS:
1. Marinate chickpeas for 15–30 minutes in the za'atar, vinegar, hemp-seed oil, lemon juice, tahini, salt, cumin, and cayenne pepper.
2. Add remaining salad ingredients. Mix and add toppings. Serve with greens.

MOROCCAN EGGPLANT SALAD
by Azzeddine Bennouna (Morocco)

Serves 4 (gluten-free)

4 medium-sized Italian eggplants, sliced
juice of 1 lemon
3 cloves garlic
1 tomato, diced
4–5 tablespoons olive oil
3 tablespoons parsley, chopped
3 tablespoons cilantro, chopped
1/2 teaspoon cumin
paprika powder to taste
salt to taste

DIRECTIONS:

1. Boil sliced eggplant in just enough water to cover it.
2. Add salt, lemon juice, and remaining ingredients. Cook until the mixture becomes pureed (you can mash it to help achieve pureed consistency).
3. Cool down and serve cold.

COWGIRL SOUTHWESTERN BEAN SALAD (gluten-free)

Tastes great with **Rise and Shine; That Breakfast Burrito Is Mine (see recipe page 72)** or **Guac N Roll (see recipe page 101)**.

Serves 8

4 cobs raw corn
4 ripe peaches, cubed
3 cups chickpeas
2 juicy mangoes, cubed
1 small onion (preferably purple), chopped
1 1/2 cups black beans
1–2 cloves garlic, chopped
juice of 1 lime
3 tablespoons apple cider vinegar
1/2 teaspoon curry powder
salt to taste
pinch of cayenne pepper
a few leaves of fresh basil, chopped
a few leaves of fresh mint, chopped
a few leaves of fresh sage, chopped

DIRECTIONS: Combine all ingredients in a big bowl until well incorporated. Set aside for 30 minutes or longer until all flavors marinate.

Ruby Red Grapefruit and Winter Spinach Salad
by Mike Geller

Mike Geller is the founder of Mike's Organic, a company based in Connecticut that delivers fresh, local, organic, and seasonal produce to your door. Mike is recognized as one of the pioneers of the farm-to-home delivery concept, with Mike's Organic Delivery being one of the first ten companies of its kind established in America. The relationships he has built within the farming community as well as his insight into the Fairfield and Westchester marketplaces have been pivotal to the growth and success of the business.

In addition, his understanding of how to work with small/local farmers and focus their efforts into a model that works for both the farmer and the consumer is unparalleled in the market. I have been using Mike's Organic services for over six years now. www.mikesorganicdelivery.com

Serves 2-4 (raw/gluten-free)

1 medium ruby red grapefruit
1 bag fresh spinach, torn
2 tablespoons scallions, chopped
2 teaspoons apple cider vinegar
2 teaspoons olive oil
2 teaspoons sweetener of your choice, such as maple syrup or coconut nectar
2 teaspoons mustard
1 pinch red pepper flakes

DIRECTIONS:

1. Make the salad: Halve grapefruit. With a sharp knife, cut around each section to loosen fruit. Reserve the juice. Toss grapefruit in a salad bowl with spinach and scallions.
2. Make the dressing: In a jar with a tight-fitting lid, combine vinegar, oil, sweetener, mustard, and reserved grapefruit juice. Shake well.
3. Drizzle dressing over salad and toss to coat. Serve immediately.

Summer Salad

by Michelle Wincze Abbruzzese

(raw/gluten-free)

Michelle Wincze Abbruzzese is a former New England Patriots Cheerleader, a breast cancer survivor, a clinical representative at a prenatal genetics lab, and the owner of Work It Dance and Fitness in Norwalk, Connecticut. Michelle actively teaches fitness classes and dance workshops across the United States and is the creator of two workout videos: Tone and Tighten and Dance Yourself Fit. You can download Michelle's workouts or check out her live class schedule by visiting her website.
www.workitfit.com

Serves 4

1 bag mesclun greens or greens of your choice
2 kiwis, peeled and sliced
1 mango
1/2 pint strawberries, halved
1/2 pint blueberries
1/2 pint raspberries

Dressing:
1/2 cup olive oil
1/2 cup freshly squeezed grapefruit juice or other citrus juice
1/2 teaspoon pink Himalayan salt
1/4 teaspoon black pepper
1 tablespoon Fines Herbs by Penzeys Spices—a mix of dried chervil, minced parsley, French tarragon, and chopped chives (feel free to use your own mix of herbs instead)
agave nectar

DIRECTIONS:

1. Make the salad: Place greens in a serving bowl. Layer the top of the greens with the fruit in the order listed above (prevents crushing the more delicate fruits).
2. Make the dressing: In a bowl, combine olive oil, juice, salt, pepper, and herbs. Whisk until well blended. Slowly add agave nectar until you achieve the sweetness you desire. Feel free to add more juice or oil to customize it to your palate.
3. Pour dressing over the salad and serve immediately, or serve with the dressing on the side.

VARIATION: For a thicker dressing, put ingredients into a blender and blend for 30 seconds on high.

Garlic and Kale Salad

by Chef Jolo

(raw/gluten-free)

Marc A. Moise, a.k.a. Chef Jolo, was born in Haiti and has been on the natural healthy eating path for over twenty-five years. He began to research and incorporate a healthy vegetarian diet while learning about the Rastafarian way of life. He opened Jolo's Kitchen and Jolo's Restaurant & Art Gallery with the intention of bringing healthy, vegan, and delicious meals and fresh juice to the Westchester County community.
Jolo's Restaurant & Art Gallery also has an event venue and full-service alcoholic bar serving vegan drinks. The event space hosts and caters public and private functions, art exhibits, and music shows.
www.JolosKitchen.com

Serves 2-4

1 big bunch fresh kale

4–5 cloves garlic, minced

1/4 cup avocado oil

juice of 1 lemon

pinch of sea salt

1/2 tablespoon agave or maple syrup

1 cucumber, sliced

1 tomato, sliced

1 avocado, sliced

DIRECTIONS:

1. Chop kale into small pieces and place in a big mixing bowl.
2. Mix garlic, avocado oil, lemon juice, and salt in a small bowl and add to kale.
3. Massage kale with your hands. Let it marinate for 20 minutes.
4. Add agave or maple syrup.
5. Serve with cucumbers, tomatoes, and avocado.

Polish Red Borscht

(gluten-free) (Poland)

This is a very popular soup in Poland, called *czerwony barszcz*. It is especially cooked in the cold months of fall and winter. This is my vegan twist on the Ukrainian version of red borscht because my hometown is Lublin, Poland, close to the border with Ukraine. The soup is easy to make. It is peasant food: healthy, flavorful, and grounding. It is perfect with fresh homemade bread. You will need a large five-quart pot for this soup.

Makes 5 quarts

16 ounces lima beans or cannellini beans

7–8 large organic beets, cubed (peel first if not organic)

7 carrots

3 sweet potatoes or 5 regular potatoes

2 parsnips

2 onions

1 cup fresh mushrooms

1/4 white cabbage

3–4 cloves of garlic

juice of 1 lemon

spices: curry powder, allspice, 3–4 bay leaves, black pepper, and whatever other spices you wish

DIRECTIONS

1. Soak the beans overnight. Rinse and cook in 4 quarts water for 30–40 minutes or until soft.
2. While the beans are cooking, chop the vegetables.
3. Add all vegetables except the cabbage and mushrooms to the pot. Cook until soft, about 10–15 minutes.
4. Add cabbage and mushrooms. If your beets came with the greens, chop them as well and add to the pot. Cook for another 5–7 minutes. Season with spices and lemon juice. I add pink Himalayan salt on the plate, not while cooking.

VARIATIONS: Serve with **Cashew Sour Cream** (see recipe page 90) or coconut cream.

• Pairs well with **Olenko's Mom's Bread** (see recipe page 98).

VEGETABLE RAMEN SOUP
(gluten-free)

You'll need to use two different pots for this recipe, one for the ramen and one for the soup.

Serves 2–4

1 (10-ounce) pack of rice ramen (I like the one from Lotus Foods. It comes in many flavors.)
2 carrots
2 sweet potatoes or purple potatoes
1/4 head of cauliflower or bunch of broccoli
1 onion
2 celery stalks
1 cup fresh shiitake mushroom (or other mushrooms), sliced
tofu (I like to use sprouted, non-GMO)
1 cup spinach
miso
3–4 nori sheets
bunch of scallions, chopped
1–2 tablespoons curry powder or spices of your choice

DIRECTIONS:

1. Prepare ramen by following instructions on package.
2. Chop carrots, potatoes, cauliflower, onion, and celery. Place in a pot with 2 quarts water. Cover and cook for about 8 minutes.
3. Add mushrooms, tofu, and spinach. Bring to a boil and turn the heat off.
4. Place the noodles in your serving bowl. Pour the soup over.
5. Scoop about 1 tablespoon of miso and mix with the soup in your bowl. Break a nori sheet and sprinkle over. Add chopped scallions and curry powder.

VARIATIONS: Season the soup with hemp seeds or sesame seeds.
• To make it spicy, add some hot sauce, such as Sriracha.
• Add any other vegetables that you like, including bok choy, cabbage, asparagus, butternut squash, kale, and Swiss chard.

VELVETY COUNTRY BUTTERNUT SQUASH BISQUE
by Natalia Levey (gluten-free)

Natalia Levey, CNC, CHC, is a professional chef, author of Cravings Boss, speaker, and certified health coach. She educates people worldwide about how to make behavioral changes resulting in improved nutrition and better energy. She is the founder of www.healthyintent.com, a company dedicated to providing healthy food and lifestyle-based solutions for weight loss, vitality, and more.

Serves 2–4

1/2 Vidalia onion, chopped
5 garlic cloves
fresh thyme
4 cups butternut squash, cubed
1 cup button mushrooms
1/3 head cauliflower
2 celery stalks, chopped
2 pears, cubed
6 cups vegetable broth
salt to taste
pepper to taste

DIRECTIONS:

1. In a stock pot, sauté onion, garlic, and thyme.
2. Add squash, mushrooms, cauliflower, and celery and sauté for 5 minutes. Add pears and vegetable broth and simmer for approximately 45 minutes until all the vegetables are tender.
3. Transfer everything to a blender (will probably be 2 batches) and purée.
4. Season with salt and pepper.

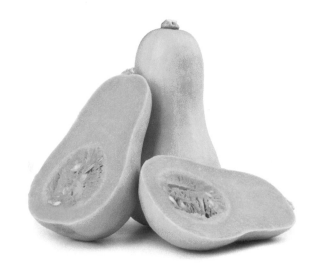

PUMPKIN SOUP
by Boshka Reid (Australia)
(gluten-free)

Boshka Reid was born in Poland and resides in Australia. She is a food and kettlebell lover who combines her passion for health and fitness with the pleasure of teaching others how to feel better in and about their bodies. You can find her online at www.boshfitpt.com, where she shares her journey. She also shares her knowledge of lifting weights at www.boshkareid.com

Serves 2–4

1–2 tablespoons coconut butter
4 cups butternut squash, chopped
1 small sweet potato, chopped
1 cup onion, chopped
2–4 cloves garlic (depending on how garlicky you like it)
1 teaspoon cinnamon
1 teaspoon ground cumin
1/2 teaspoon ground nutmeg
1–2 pinches cayenne pepper (optional)
2–4 cups homemade vegetable stock or water
1 tablespoon coconut cream per person, for serving
cilantro, for garnish

DIRECTIONS:

1. In a large pot, melt coconut butter. Add squash and sweet potato and cook until lightly brown.
2. Add onion and garlic. Stir and cook until translucent.
3. Add spices and 2 cups of stock (or water if you don't have any homemade vegetable stock) and simmer until potato and pumpkin are soft.
4. Cool soup and blend with a stick blender. Add more stock if the consistency is too thick.
5. Serve with a swirl of coconut cream through the middle and sprinkle with chopped cilantro.

VARIATION: Use 1 chopped jalapeño in place of cayenne pepper. Add it to cooking soup prior to blending.

SQUASH YOUR CARROTS AWAY SOUP
by Bronwyn Frazier-Miller
(gluten-free)

Bronwyn Frazier-Miller is an artist and photographer who loves the outdoors and enjoys making healthy and tasty food recipes. She currently lives with her husband, Ben, and their cat in Westchester County, New York.
www.facebook.com/bronwynfrazier/

Serves 4-6

coconut oil, enough to cook onion, shallot, garlic, and turmeric
1/2 onion
1 medium-sized shallot
2 cloves garlic, minced
1 (1 1/2-inch) piece turmeric
6 cups vegetable broth
1 pound carrots, peeled and chopped
1 1/2 cups peeled and chopped butternut squash
1 1/2 teaspoons cumin
1/2 –1 teaspoon curry
1/4 teaspoon cardamom
1 teaspoon coriander
1/4 teaspoon ginger
2 tablespoons cilantro, plus more for garnish
1 tablespoon brown sugar
juice and grated peel of 1 organic lime
1/8 teaspoon cinnamon
1/8 teaspoon allspice
1 1/2 teaspoons pink Himalayan salt or sea salt

DIRECTIONS:

1. Heat coconut oil in a pot and add onion, shallot, garlic, and turmeric. Sauté for about 2 minutes or until the onion becomes clear.
2. Add vegetable broth, carrots, squash, cumin, curry, cardamom, coriander, and ginger. Simmer for 30 minutes.
3. Add cilantro, brown sugar, salt, lime peel, lime juice, cinnamon, and allspice.
4. Transfer to a blender or use an immersion blender and blend until smooth.
5. Garnish with more cilantro and serve.

Oh, Baby Baby Lima Bean Soup

(gluten-free)

Makes 5 quarts

1 pound baby lima beans, soaked overnight

3 sweet potatoes, chopped

1 small butternut squash or pumpkin, peeled and cut up

1 large onion, chopped

1 head garlic, chopped

1 small bunch kale

Cashew Sour Cream (see recipe page 90)

DIRECTIONS:

1. Cook presoaked baby lima beans for about 20–30 minutes or until soft.

2. Add potatoes, squash, onion, and garlic to cooked beans.

3. Cook for about 5 minutes longer and add kale. Bring to a boil and turn the heat off.

4. Serve with **Cashew Sour Cream.**

NOT CORNY BUT CREAMY CORN SOUP (raw/gluten-free)

Serves 2

3 cups raw or frozen sweet corn (more if you like thicker soup)
1 cup pure water
1 clove garlic
1/3 teaspoon salt
1 tablespoon hemp seed oil
pinch of cayenne pepper

DIRECTIONS: Mix all ingredients in a high-speed blender.

VARIATIONS: Serve with fresh herbs-such as cilantro, scallions, or parsley-or serve with **That's So Cheesy Vegan Macadamia Cheese (see recipe page 86)** or **Macadamia Nut Ricotta Cheese (see recipe page 87)**.

CAULIFLOWER MOUSSE
by Sandra Bolognia (gluten-free)

Sandra Bolognia is a teacher, artist, counselor, and spiritual advisor who studied raw food and nutrition for twenty years. Sandra makes jewelry that holds essential oils, which assists her in helping others reach their highest potential. She learned how to incorporate essential oils into her lifestyle for healing and feels that she has finally grasped how to combine foods to taste delicious. www.SandraBolognia.com

Serves 1–2

1 head cauliflower
1/2 cup coconut cream or unsweetened non-dairy coffee cream
2 tablespoons olive oil
1/2 teaspoon pink Himalayan salt
1/4 to 1/2 teaspoon onion powder
pepper to taste

DIRECTIONS:

1. Clean and break cauliflower into natural pieces. Steam until a fork easily pierces it.
2. Drain cauliflower and place in a high-speed blender. Add remaining ingredients and blend until smooth.
3. Serve with veggies or as a soup.

Healthy Lentil Soup
by Rebecca Phillippo (gluten-free)

Rebecca Phillippo is a certified Pilates practitioner and founder of Forward Movement Lifestyle Pilates Studio in Pleasantville, New York. While the studio is her main priority, cycling plays a huge part in her overall healthy lifestyle. In 2010, Rebecca was diagnosed with stage 3 invasive breast cancer. Pilates was integral in helping her recover and build strength and confidence back in her body after surgeries and intense treatments. Rebecca is currently cancer-free and racing her mountain bike any chance she gets. www.fmlifestyleinc.com

Serves 4

1/2 cup olive oil
1 onion, chopped
3–4 cloves garlic, chopped
4–5 carrots, diced
4–5 stalks of celery, diced
1 1/2 teaspoons salt
1 teaspoon pepper
1 1/2 teaspoons turmeric
1 tablespoon oregano or rosemary
1 cup dried red lentils
sriracha sauce

DIRECTIONS:

1. Cover the bottom of a medium-size pot with a thin layer of olive oil. Heat over medium heat. Sauté onion and garlic for 5 minutes.
2. Add carrots and sauté for another 5 minutes. Add celery, salt, and pepper (I prefer kosher salt and freshly ground pepper). Add turmeric and oregano and continue to simmer for 7–10 minutes.
3. Add 5 cups water and lentils. Bring to a boil. Cover and simmer for 30–40 minutes.
4. Remove from heat. Use a blender to blend the ingredients together.
5. If desired, add sriracha to taste to each serving, depending on how spicy you like it.

CHAPTER 13

Life Is Short. Eat Dessert First.
Sweets That Are So Yummy That They Will
Make You Sing in Your Tummy!

You can have your cake and eat it too! These desserts are healthy and guilt-free. Enjoy them for breakfast or any time of the day. There are no rules with my rainbow diet when you make healthy, plant-based dishes.

FRUITY FRUIT POPSICLES
(raw/gluten-free)

Mangoes, strawberries,
persimmons, bananas,
or other fruit of your choice

DIRECTIONS:

1. Add fruit to a high-speed blender and mix.
2. Pour mixture into popsicle molds and place in the freezer.
3. To add different colors to your popsicles, take popsicles out of freezer after 15 minutes. Mix additional fruit and pour on top. Place popsicles back in the freezer until frozen.

VARIATIONS: Add a little bit of coconut water, nut milk, or coconut milk to make the popsicles creamier.
  • Slice fruit like kiwi or strawberries, place them in popsicle molds, and pour in coconut water, coconut milk, or nut milk. Place in freezer. If you like your popsicles sweeter, add very ripe bananas or watermelon.

I'm Not Going to Deny That I Love the Sweet Cherry Pie

(raw/gluten-free)

Serves 12-14

Crust:

3 cups Medjool dates, pitted

2 cups pecans

mulberries (optional)

1 tablespoon pumpkin spice (cardamom, cinnamon, ginger, nutmeg, vanilla)

Filling:

3 cups raw cashews

1 cup coconut water plus 1 cup filtered water (or could be 2 cups of the same water)

1 banana

4 tablespoons sweetener: maple syrup, agave, coconut nectar, or yacon syrup

1 dropper vanilla extract

16 ounces frozen cherries

DIRECTIONS:

1. Make the crust: Pulse all crust ingredients in a food processor until dough becomes sticky. If it is too soft, place it in the fridge for a while to set. Transfer crust to a pie dish and press hard to the bottom.

2. Make the filling: Blend cashews, water, banana, sweetener, and vanilla in a high-speed blender until smooth.

3. Pour filling mixture on top of crust and add frozen cherries. You may leave cherries visible on top or press in to hide.

4. Place in the freezer for 4–6 hours. Leave out for several minutes before serving.

VARIATION: If you want to add color to your pie, use natural food coloring, such as Blue Chai Flower Tea or Blue Majik. Drizzle over the pie and make swirls for a visual effect.

• You may also place dried fruit on top, such as strawberries, raspberries, or cherries.

Pumpkin Lovers' Cake

by Marina Jacobi (gluten-free)

Marina Jacobi was born in Bulgaria but currently resides in the United States. She works in the field of quantum physics, higher consciousness, parallel realities, and other dimensions. She has been on a plant-based diet for several years. She enjoys making healthy dishes for her family using organic, non-GMO ingredients. Marina created this recipe for her son who has celiac disease. To learn more about Marina and her work, visit her website. www.marinajacobi.com

Serves 8-10
2 cups almond flour
1/2 cup pumpkin purée
1/2 cup coconut milk
1 teaspoon vanilla extract
1 tablespoon coconut oil
1 teaspoon baking powder
1 teaspoon baking soda
1/2 teaspoon cinnamon
1/2 teaspoon nutmeg
1-2 ripe bananas
10 soaked Medjool dates, pitted

DIRECTIONS:
1. Preheat oven to 400°F.
2. Soak dates in water for 1 hour. Don't discard the water; you may need it later if the dough is too thick.
3. Place flour in a mixing bowl.
4. Add the rest of the ingredients to a high-speed blender and mix until smooth.
5. Combine the blended mixture with the flour and mix well.
6. Coat a baking pan with coconut oil and line with parchment paper. Fold in the mixture and bake at 400°F for about 40-50 minutes, depending on your oven.

VARIATION: Add 1/2 cup raisins and 1/2 cup walnuts for a sweeter and crunchier taste.

SWEET GOOEY DEWY CHEWY FRUIT ROLL-UPS
(raw/gluten-free)

3-4 cups fresh sweet strawberries, raspberries, blueberries, pineapple, pear, mango, banana, or any other fruit of your choice
1-2 tablespoons fresh lemon, lime, or orange juice (optional)

DIRECTIONS:
1. Puree fruit in a high-speed blender. If you like, you can add the fruit juice to enhance the flavor.
2. Pour the pureed fruit on dehydrator Teflon sheets or parchment paper. Spread a thin layer with a spatula or a spoon to make even on top.
3. Dehydrate at 118°F for 8 hours or more. If it doesn't peel off easily, dehydrate a little longer.
4. When the fruit roll has dried, peel from the sheet, cut in desired sizes, and roll tightly. You can place the small-size parchment paper over the fruit roll-up before rolling to prevent from sticking.

VARIATIONS: Use this recipe to create ice-cream cones. Halfway into the dehydration, roll them into cone shapes and dehydrate until crispy. Serve with **You May Be Surprised, But This Ice Cream Tastes So Nice (see recipe page 131).**
 • This recipe can be used to make raw vegan crepes. For the filling, use **Cashew Sour Cream (see recipe page 90)** or fruit sorbet.

CHOCOLATE LOVERS' BANANA ICE-CREAM POPSICLES
(raw/gluten-free)

This is a healthy, easy, raw, vegan, gluten-free, and delicious alternative to ice cream that you can make at home for your children. It tastes amazing, and kids and adults love it!

Serves 8-10
Popsicles:
4 large ripe bananas
wooden ice-cream sticks or plastic straws
3-4 tablespoons coconut oil
6 tablespoons raw cacao powder

1–2 tablespoons maple syrup
Toppings:
raw cacao nibs, chia seeds, goji berries, peanut or almond butter, peanuts or raw jungle peanuts, **Unicorn Rainbow Magical Sprinkles (see recipe page 148).**

DIRECTIONS:
1. Cut unpeeled bananas in half. If they are very long, cut them in thirds. Peel the skin off.
2. Place straws or sticks in the middle of each banana. If the straws are too long, trim them a bit. Freeze bananas for a few hours or overnight.
3. While the bananas are in the freezer, melt coconut oil in a double boiler. Add raw cacao. The temperature should be 95–98°F and not too hot to your touch. Keep mixing with a spoon. Add maple syrup. When the texture is smooth, remove from heat.
4. Dip each frozen banana in the chocolate. Use a spoon to spread the chocolate evenly.
5. Decorate popsicles with toppings. Serve immediately or put back in the freezer in a glass dish. They will stay fresh for many weeks.

CHERRY VANILLA ICE CREAM
(raw/gluten-free)

Serves 2
Ice cream:
4 very ripe bananas, frozen
2 Medjool dates, pitted
1/2 teaspoon vanilla powder
1/2 cup frozen, fresh, or dried pitted cherries
Toppings:
fresh coconut meat, frozen berries, pomegranate, strawberries, plantain chips, sweet pea shoots, or cacao nibs

DIRECTIONS:
1. Place bananas, dates, and vanilla in a high-speed blender and blend until smooth.
2. Transfer mixture to a glass container. Add cherries and swirl. Store in freezer.
3. Serve with your favorite toppings.

YOU MAY BE SURPRISED, BUT THIS ICE CREAM TASTES SO NICE
(raw/gluten-free)

Serves 2
4–5 very ripe bananas, frozen
2–3 Medjool dates, pitted
1/2 teaspoon vanilla powder

DIRECTIONS:
1. Place bananas, dates, and vanilla in a high-speed blender and blend until smooth.
2. Transfer mixture to a glass container. Store in freezer.
3. When frozen, scoop out with an ice-cream scoop. Serve in a tall glass garnished with your favorite toppings.

VARIATIONS: To create different color ice cream, refer to the natural pigments guidelines **on page 67.**
• To create fun ice-cream sandwiches, use any cookie and any ice cream recipe in this book.
• You can make your own sorbet by placing frozen fruit of your choice and blending it in a high-speed blender.
• For a creamier texture of your ice-cream, use an ice-cream maker.

Guilt-Free Peanut Butter Cups

(raw/gluten-free)

Serves 12-14

Raw Chocolate:

1 cup raw cacao butter

5 tablespoons coconut oil

1 1/2 cups raw cacao powder

5 tablespoons maple syrup (or more if you prefer sweeter chocolate)

1 tablespoon lucuma powder

1/2 teaspoon Medicine Flower Vanilla or vanilla extract or powder

pinch pink Himalayan salt, plus more for sprinkling

pinch cayenne pepper

Filling:

Peanut butter or any other nut butter you like, such as almond, cashew, or hazelnut

DIRECTIONS:

1. In a double boiler, melt cacao butter and coconut oil over very low heat, about 105–110°F.

2. Add cacao powder and mix slowly with a wooden spoon.

3. Add remaining chocolate ingredients and keep mixing until perfectly smooth.

4. Fill chocolate molds, paper, or silicone cups halfway with chocolate mixture, and then add a scoop of raw nut butter. Finish the cups with another layer of chocolate.

5. Place in the refrigerator to set. You can sprinkle some salt on top. Store in a glass container in the refrigerator, or freeze for up to 8 weeks. .

Chocolate Bliss Cake with Avocado Mousse

(raw)

Serves 10-12

Dough:

1 cup gluten-free oats

1 cup raw cashews

1/2 cup raw almonds

2 cups Medjool dates, pitted and soaked for 2 hours

4 tablespoons raw cacao powder

1/2 teaspoon Ceylon cinnamon

1/2 teaspoon vanilla powder

1/2 teaspoon ginger powder

1/2 teaspoon cardamom powder

pinch salt

Filling:

1 cup shredded coconut

3-4 bananas

Avocado Chocolate Mousse:

2 ripe avocados

1 tablespoon maple syrup

5 tablespoons water

1 teaspoon orange blossom water

1/2 teaspoon vanilla powder

3 tablespoons carob powder

1 tablespoon raw cacao powder

pinch salt

fresh raspberries and mint, for decorating

DIRECTIONS:

1. Make the dough: Place oats, cashews, and almonds in a food processor and mix until smooth. Add the remaining ingredients and process until you achieve a dough-like consistency. You may have to stop and scrape the sides.

2. Divide the dough mixture into two even portions. Fold one part into a springform cake pan.

3. Make the filling: Slice bananas and place them on the first layer of the cake in the pan. Sprinkle in some shredded coconut. Fold in the second part of the dough.

4. Place cake in freezer for 1–2 hours to set while you make the mousse.

5. Make the mousse: Place all mousse ingredients in a high-speed blender and mix until smooth.

6. Finish: Layer the mousse on top of the cake. Sprinkle on more shredded coconut. Decorate with fresh raspberries, mint, and lime or lemon zest.

Super Natural Carrot Truffles

by Christina Leidenheimer
(raw/gluten-free)

Christina Leidenheimer, CPT, CPI, CNC, is a plant-based raw-food enthusiast, passionate Pilates instructor, and certified detoxification specialist (ISOD). Through her magazine, Healthy Works, and her latest book, Super-Natural Juicing, Christina is exploring and reporting all things related to natural health and wellness.
www.naturallychristina.com

Serve 12
1 cup pecans
1 large carrot
1 cup raisins
2 tablespoons raw coconut flakes
1/2 tablespoon coconut oil
dash cinnamon
dash pink Himalayan salt

DIRECTIONS:
1. Soak pecans in water for 8 hours. Strain and set aside.
2. Wash and peel carrot. Cut into chunks.
3. Add soaked pecans, carrot chunks, and all remaining ingredients to food processor. Pulse on high for 1 minute. Mixture should turn into a ball. Scrape sides as needed.
4. Remove the blade from the food processor. Take 1 tablespoon of the mixture at a time and form into balls. Continue until all mixture is used.
5. Place balls in a refrigerator for 15 minutes before serving.

LEMON COCONUT BALLS
by Skye Nixon (Australia)
(raw/gluten-free)

**Skye Nixon lives in Australia, and she is a passionate beauty therapist, Reiki therapist, and yoga teacher. She promotes the concept of self-love through rituals of self-care. She aims to remind others of their truth by connecting them to their heart space via yoga, body work, meditation, and mentoring.
www.ritualsofselflove.com**

Serves 30
30 Medjool dates, soaked and pitted
1 1/4 cups shredded coconut, divided
1 teaspoon pure vanilla paste, powder, or extract
1 large lemon—all of the rind and half of the juice

DIRECTIONS:
1. Place the dates, 3/4 cup of the coconut, and the vanilla paste into a food processor and process until the mixture starts to combine and become smoother in texture.
2. Add the lemon juice and rind. Process until smooth and combined. Taste the mixture and add more rind to your taste.
3. Use your hands to roll the mixture into balls and then into the remaining 1/2 cup coconut. Make them your desired snack size and store in the freezer for a quick sweet snack. They will last for months—if you don't eat them all at once.

VARIATION: Make these coconut balls orange-flavored by replacing the lemon with an orange.

CHUNKY MONKEY COOKIES
by Yvonne Ardestani

Chef Yvonne is a classically trained French chef, former restaurant cook under chefs Suzanne Goin and Breanne Varela, and now a wellness chef. She develops vegan and gluten-free versions of the classics and of recipes she learned in culinary school and professional restaurants. All of her recipes are vegan; gluten-, soy-, and dairy-free; and best of all, devoid of refined ingredients. Yvonne is very passionate about and dedicated to promoting

a healthier lifestyle and nutrition, helping the environment, and protecting animals from cruelty while still eating deliciously. She currently owns and operates the Yvonne's Vegan Kitchen wholesale line of vegan sweets and treats, offering goods to over twenty locations in Los Angeles.
www.myeclectickitchen.com

Serves 14
1 1/2 large ripe bananas, peeled
1/4 cup creamy peanut butter or sunflower butter
1 tablespoon flax meal
1 tablespoon coconut nectar or maple syrup
2 teaspoons vanilla extract
1 1/2 teaspoons applesauce
1 1/4 cups rolled gluten-free oats
6 tablespoons vegan chocolate chunks or chips
4 tablespoons walnuts, chopped
1/2 teaspoon baking powder
1/8 teaspoon ground cinnamon
1/8 teaspoon sea salt

DIRECTIONS:
1. Preheat oven to 350°F.
2. In a medium bowl, mash the bananas and add the peanut butter, flax meal, coconut nectar, vanilla extract, and applesauce. Mix well and set aside.
3. In a small bowl, combine the remaining ingredients and mix.
4. Add the wet ingredients to the dry ingredients and mix thoroughly to combine. Allow the batter to sit for 15 minutes.
5. Using a 1-ounce ice-cream scoop or by measuring out heaping tablespoons, scoop out cookies onto a half sheet pan lined with parchment paper or a silpat mat. Flatten the tops of the cookies with your hand or a spatula. Bake for 12–14 minutes or until golden.
6. Allow cookies to sit on the baking sheet for at least 3 minutes before transferring to a wire rack to cool.

CHOCOLATE AND ALMOND BISCOTTI by Joan Cosentino (Italy)

Joan Cosentino has been teaching elementary school for many years. Her love of cooking and baking stems from her upbringing in a home with parents and family who immigrated to the United States from Italy many years ago. The kitchen was the central part of the home. Homegrown vegetables from a summer garden, a yearly tradition of canning tomato sauce, and kneading dough for pizza and bread have always been an important part of her life. Joan continues the tradition of creating dishes using family recipes that have been handed down through the years, bringing memories back to life. This traditional Italian recipe has been veganized by Aleksandra and Joan. The biscotti are delicious served with espresso, latte, or cappuccino.

Serves 35
6 tablespoons flax seeds or flaxseed meal
2 cups whole-wheat flour
1 cup almonds, shredded or sliced
1 cup vegan chocolate chips
1/2 cup coconut sugar
1/2 cup raisins
4 tablespoons maple syrup
3 tablespoons anise seed
3 tablespoons coconut oil, melted
3 tablespoons anisette or rum
2 tablespoons lemon juice
2 tablespoons vanilla extract
2 teaspoons almond extract
1 teaspoon cinnamon
1 teaspoon baking powder
1/2 teaspoon cardamom
dash salt

DIRECTIONS:
1. Preheat oven to 300°F.
2. Mix flax seeds with 11 tablespoons water and set aside.
3. Combine flax seeds and all remaining ingredients in a bowl and mix. Divide dough in half.
4. On a greased and floured baking sheet, pat dough into two logs, each about 1/2 inch thick, 1 1/2 inches wide, and 12 inches long, spaced about 2 inches apart.
5. Bake for about 40 minutes or until golden brown. Cool for about 5 minutes.
6. Place on a cutting board and, with a serrated knife, slice diagonally at a 45-degree angle, about 1/2 inch thick. Lay slices flat on a baking sheet and return to a 275-degree oven for 20 to 25 minutes, turning over once to dry the other side.

VARIATION: Melt chocolate and drizzle over the biscotti. Allow to cool and harden.

ALMOND OATMEAL RAISIN COOKIES

Serves 20

3 cups almond flour
2 cups oats
1 cup raisins
1 cup pumpkin or sunflower seeds
3/4 cup coconut milk
1 tablespoon fresh lemon juice
1 teaspoon vanilla powder
1 teaspoon Ceylon cinnamon
1 teaspoon ginger
1/2 teaspoon nutmeg
1/2 teaspoon baking powder

DIRECTIONS:

1. Preheat oven to 350°F.
2. Combine all ingredients in a bowl and mix gently.
3. Scoop out dough and form cookies.
4. Grease a baking sheet with coconut oil. Place cookies on baking sheet, spacing them apart. Bake for 45 minutes or until golden.

VARIATION: You can add vegan chocolate chips to this recipe.

CHA-CHA-CHA CHIA COOKIES

Serves 12–14

1 cup chia seeds
10–12 ripe bananas
1 cup coconut shreds
1 cup oats
2/3 cup amaranth flour
1/2 cup raisins
4 tablespoons coconut sugar
2 tablespoons molasses
2 tablespoons maple syrup
1 1/2 tablespoons pumpkin spice

DIRECTIONS:

1. Preheat oven to 350°F.
2. Combine chia seeds with 2 cups water and set aside for a few minutes to form a chia egg.
3. Mash bananas with a fork until you achieve a smooth consistency.
4. Combine chia seeds, bananas, and all remaining ingredients in a big bowl and gently mix.
5. Scoop out the dough and form cookies with your hands.
6. Place cookies on a greased baking sheet and bake for about 45 minutes.

PUMPKIN AMARANTH FLOUR MUFFINS

Serves 9

1 1/2 tablespoons coconut oil
2 ripe bananas, mashed with a fork
1 1/2 cups amaranth flour
1 cup canned pumpkin
1/2 cup walnuts
1/2 cup raisins
5 tablespoons coconut or brown sugar
4 tablespoons oats
1 tablespoon cinnamon
1 tablespoon ginger (or more)
1 tablespoon flax seeds
1 teaspoon baking powder
1/2 teaspoon nutmeg
1/2 teaspoon baking soda

DIRECTIONS:

1. Preheat oven to 350°F.
2. Melt coconut oil in a double boiler.
3. Place melted coconut oil and all remaining ingredients in a bowl and gently mix together.
4. Grease paper muffin forms. Fold the batter into the forms and place in a muffin baking sheet. Bake for about 45 minutes or until done. To check if the muffins are ready, insert a wooden toothpick into one. If there is wet dough on the toothpick, the muffins are not ready. If the toothpick comes out clean, the muffins are ready.

VARIATION: Use this recipe to make delicious cookies.

Merry Berry Summer Cake
(raw/gluten-free)

Serves 10

Crust:
2 cups Medjool dates, pitted
1/3 cup dried mulberries
1/2 cup raw walnuts or pecans

Filling:
3 cups raw cashews (soaked in filtered water for
3–4 hours)
1 cup raw coconut water or coconut milk
2 large ripe bananas
5 tablespoons maple syrup
3 tablespoons coconut cream
2 tablespoons lucuma powder (optional)
2 tablespoons dried mulberries
1 tablespoon fresh lemon juice
1 1/2 cups raspberries (or other berries) for the
filling, plus another ½–1 cup for garnish

DIRECTIONS:

1. Make crust: Process all crust ingredients in a food processor. Press to the bottom of a medium springform pan.
2. Make the filling: Mix all ingredients except the berries in a high-speed blender or food processor.
3. Pour filling mixture over crust. Add the berries, either whole or blended in a high-speed blender, and then pour over the filling and gently swirl in. If you prefer, you may layer the colors by alternating between the white filling and the fruit layer.
4. Freeze for about 8 hours or overnight. Decorate with the remaining berries.
5. Take the cake out of the freezer half an hour before serving.

VARIATIONS: You can also decorate the cake with edible flowers, caramel, lemon zest, **Unicorn Rainbow Magical Sprinkles (see recipe page 148)**, or **Cashew Buttercream Frosting (see recipe page 151).** Experiment with different flavors.
 • Replace the berries with any other fruit that is in season. Just make sure to use ripe fruit, or you will need to add more sweetener.

Another option is to make a rainbow cake. Divide
the filling among several bowls and add natural
food colorings to each part (see color suggestions
on page 66-67). You may also make individual
cakes using cupcake forms. Making this cake is
just like painting when you mix and experiment
with your own colors. It is a fun activity to do
with children.

Raw Baklava Shake

by Ana Palacios-Sampaio
(raw/gluten-free)

Anna Palacios-Sampaio was born and raised in Ecuador but now lives in New Jersey. She is a registered nurse and a nutrition and wellness coach. She has a strong love and passion for the knowledge and application of health principles in disease prevention through diet and lifestyle management as well as the use of simple, natural remedies. You can visit her at Facebook at Ana. Palacios Sampaio or Pinterest at Fresh_and_Raw

Serves 1-2
2 large ripe bananas, frozen
5 Medjool dates, pitted
1 cup almond milk
1/4 cup pistachios
2 tablespoons sweetener of your choice, such as maple syrup, agave, or coconut nectar
1/4 teaspoon ground cloves
1/4 teaspoon cardamom
1/4 teaspoon Ceylon cinnamon
pinch sea salt

DIRECTIONS: Place all ingredients in a high-speed blender and blend to a smooth consistency. You may blend in some ice if you like. Drink to your heart health.

GREEN DRAGON AVOCADO ICE CREAM
(raw/gluten-free)

Serves 2-4
2 ripe avocados
1 ripe banana
1/2 ripe mango
1 cup baby spinach
2 tablespoons maple syrup
pinch salt
raw cacao nibs or crumbled raw chocolate, for topping

DIRECTIONS:
1. Place avocados, banana, mango, spinach, syrup, and salt in a high-speed blender and process until smooth.
2. Transfer mixture to a glass container. Add raw cacao nibs or chocolate. Store in freezer.

PUMPKIN TRUFFLES
(raw/gluten-free)

Serves 15-20
2 cups Medjool dates, pitted (soak first if dry)
2 cups pecans
1/2 cup raw cacao nibs
1 can pumpkin puree
1 tablespoon cinnamon
1/2 teaspoon cardamom
1/2 teaspoon ginger
pinch black pepper
shredded coconut (optional)

DIRECTIONS:
1. Place dates and pecans in a food processor and mix until smooth.
2. Add remaining ingredients and pulse.
3. Scoop out the mixture and form small balls with your hands. Roll in shredded coconut flakes or cacao powder, if desired.
4. Store in glass container in refrigerator or freeze for later.

SPICED-UP GINGERSNAP BISCOTTI (gluten-free)

Biscotti are delicious with tea or coffee.

Serves 24
2 1/2 cups almond flour
1 cup sliced almonds
1/2 cup chopped candied ginger
1/2 cup raisins
6 tablespoons pumpkin puree
2 tablespoons coconut sugar
2 tablespoons Sambuca
1–2 tablespoons molasses
1 tablespoon raw coconut nectar
1 tablespoon rose water or orange blossom water
1 tablespoon pure almond extract
1 tablespoon anise
1 tablespoon melted coconut oil
1 tablespoon maple syrup
1 1/2 teaspoons ginger powder
1 1/2 teaspoons Ceylon cinnamon
1 1/2 teaspoons cardamom
1 teaspoon flax seeds
1/2 teaspoon baking soda
1/2 teaspoon vanilla powder
1/4 teaspoon sea salt or pink Himalayan salt

DIRECTIONS:
1. Preheat oven to 350°F.
2. Combine all ingredients in a big bowl and mix gently. You may want to use your hands.
3. On a parchment paper, pat out dough into two logs, each about 1/2 inch thick, 1 1/2 inches wide, and 12 inches long. Place on a baking sheet, spaced about 2 inches apart, and bake for about 30 minutes. Remove from oven and allow to cool.
4. Cut the biscotti on the diagonal into 1/2-inch slices. Reduce oven to 300°F. Place cut biscotti back in the oven for additional 20 minutes or longer, depending on desired texture.

CHICKPEA FLOUR MUFFINS (gluten-free)

Serves 12
1 1/2 cups water
1 1/2 cups amaranth flour
1 1/4 cups chickpea flour
2 bananas
3 tablespoons coconut palm sugar
2 tablespoons flax seeds
1 tablespoon chia seeds
1 teaspoon aluminum-free baking powder
1 teaspoon baking soda
1 teaspoon cinnamon
pinch cardamom
pinch ginger
1 cup mixed nuts (almond, sunflower seeds, pumpkin seeds, raisins)

DIRECTIONS:
1. Preheat oven to 350°F.
2. Place all ingredients except the nuts in a food processor and mix. Add the nuts and pulse.
3. Grease a muffin pan with coconut oil or use muffin liners. Spoon mixture into a muffin pan.
4. Bake for 45 minutes or until a toothpick inserted into center of a muffin comes out clean.

Cosmic Oatmeal Cookies and Donuts

Makes 15 Cookies & 6 Donuts

Dough:

2 ripe bananas

2 cups water

1 1/2 cups oats

3/4 cup millet flour

1/2 cup flaxseed meal

1/2 cup shredded coconut

1/2 cup raisins

1/2 cup sunflower seeds

5 tablespoons coconut sugar

3 tablespoons melted coconut oil

1 tablespoon molasses

1 tablespoon pumpkin spice powder

1 tablespoon baking powder

pinch salt

2 cups vegan chocolate chips

Cosmic Glaze:

1 cup cashews

beet powder or a piece of fresh beet for red glaze

turmeric for yellow glaze

purple cabbage for purple glaze

lemon juice for pink glaze

matcha green tea powder or spirulina
for green glaze

DIRECTIONS:

1. Preheat oven to 350°F.

2. Make the dough: Place all dough ingredients except the chocolate chips in a bowl and mix together. Divide the batter in half.

3. Make the cookies: Add chocolate chips to one dough half. Form about 15 cookies and place them on a baking sheet.

4. Make the donuts: Fold dough into a donut bake sheet to make about 6 donuts.

5. Bake: Place the cookies and donuts in the oven. Bake for about 45 minutes or more, until they are done.

6. Make the glaze: Mix cashews with 1 cup water in a high-speed blender. Let sit in refrigerator for about 2 hours.

7. Color the glaze: Divide glaze into 4 small bowls. For red glaze, add beet powder or a piece of fresh beet, and blend with the cashews in a blender. For yellow glaze, add turmeric. For purple glaze, add a leaf of purple cabbage. If you want it pink, add some lemon juice. For green glaze, add matcha green tea powder or spirulina.

8. Drizzle the glaze over the donuts right before serving. You can freeze them in a glass container to enjoy later.

BEAN YOURSELF BROWNIES

Serves 12

3 (15.5-ounce) cans black beans, mashed
4 large ripe bananas, mashed
1 cup walnuts, pecans, or almonds
3/4 cup raw cacao powder
1/2 cup dried cherries, raisins, or mulberries
6 tablespoons maple syrup
3 tablespoons water
3 tablespoons oats
2 tablespoons coconut oil
1 tablespoon date or coconut sugar
1 1/2 teaspoons cinnamon
1 teaspoon vanilla powder
pinch salt

DIRECTIONS:
1. Preheat oven to 350°F.
2. Mix all ingredients in a big bowl.
3. Grease a baking dish with coconut oil or line with parchment paper.
4. Fold mixture into baking dish and bake for 30 minutes.
5. Serve warm or refrigerate and serve cold.

VARIATION: Add a layer of raw chocolate on top **(see recipe for Unicorn Brownies, page 147).**
• If you have a sweet tooth, add more sweetener.
• Use six cups cooked beans instead of canned.

GOOEY SWEET POTATO BROWNIES

Serves 12

1 cup cooked sweet potatoes, pressed tightly in a measuring cup
1 cup oat flour
1 cup vegan chocolate chips
1/2 cup raw cacao powder
1/2 cup almond butter
1/4 cup coconut sugar
1 teaspoon vanilla powder
1/2 teaspoon cinnamon
1 1/2 teaspoons baking soda
1/4 teaspoon pink Himalayan salt

DIRECTIONS:
1. Preheat oven to 300–325°F.
2. Mix all ingredients in a big bowl or a food processor.
3. Line a glass baking dish with parchment paper. Fold in the batter and bake for 20–25 minutes.
4. Serve warm right out of the oven with **You May Be Surprised, But This Ice Cream Tastes So Nice (see recipe page 131)** or put in a refrigerator and serve cold.

VARIATIONS: If you don't have oat flour, simply process gluten-free oats in a high-speed blender until you achieve a flour-like consistency.
• These brownies are sweet. If you prefer, you can use less coconut sugar or 5–6 soaked Medjool dates instead.

CRISPY CHOCOLATE OATMEAL CHICKPEA COOKIES A.K.A. OOPS COOKIES

Serves 20

3 cups oatmeal
2 bananas, mashed
1 1/2 cups chickpea flour
1 cup coconut sugar
1 cup cacao powder
1/2 cup sunflower seeds
1/2 cup mulberries
1/2 cup dried cherries
1/2 cup pumpkin seeds
1/2 cup water
1/3 cup molasses
1/3 cup coconut oil
2 tablespoons chia seeds
1 teaspoon cardamom
1 teaspoon cinnamon
1 teaspoon vanilla powder
1/2 teaspoon pink Himalayan salt
1/2 teaspoon baking powder

DIRECTIONS:
1. Preheat oven to 350°F.
2. Mix all ingredients in a big bowl. Scoop out and form cookies.
3. Grease a baking sheet with coconut oil. Place cookies on baking sheet, spacing them apart. Bake for 30 minutes.

UNICORN BROWNIES
(raw/gluten-free)

Serves 12

Brownies:

2 1/2 cups Medjool dates, pitted

1 1/2 cups walnuts or pecans

1/2 cup raw cacao powder

1/2 cup dried mulberries or raisins

1/2 tablespoon rose water (optional)

1/2 teaspoon cinnamon

Raw Chocolate Layer:

4 tablespoons coconut oil

1/2 cup raw cacao powder

3–4 tablespoons maple syrup

1 dropper Medicine Flower Vanilla or 2 tablespoons vanilla extract

pinch pink Himalayan salt

Unicorn Rainbow Magical Sprinkles (see recipe page 148), for topping

DIRECTIONS:

1. Make the brownies: Process all ingredients in a food processor until batter is all combined and sticky. Line a glass dish with parchment paper and fold in the batter. Press hard with a spoon or fork.

2. Make the raw chocolate layer: Melt coconut oil in a double boiler and add remaining ingredients. Mix until you achieve a smooth consistency. Add more sweetener if you like sweeter chocolate.

3. Spread chocolate evenly on top of brownies. Use a spatula to smooth out. Add sprinkles. Place in refrigerator to set.

4. When brownies become firm, cut into squares and enjoy. Keep in the refrigerator or freezer for a few weeks.

VARIATION: Experiment with flavors and use orange blossom water, vanilla extract, or almond extract.

Unicorn Rainbow Magical Sprinkles

(raw/gluten-free)

I am an artist and a painter. For me, painting is relaxing and fun. I love to experiment and invent my own colors while painting.

When I create colorful, healthy raw and baked desserts, I love to decorate them with magical sprinkles. These sprinkles will turn any smoothie, ice cream, waffle, pancake, cookie, cake, or parfait into a true masterpiece. Let your imagination run wild to create your colors.

In prehistoric times, cavemen used natural pigments from the earth to paint the walls of caves, so we can say that this technique is very old. Today's paint is all synthetic, and what is even worse is that food colorings are made with harsh chemicals. This is why I invented these fun unicorn rainbow sprinkles. They are great to make with your children and grandchildren, or with friends at children's birthday parties. Adults will enjoy this sprinkle-making time too.

All you need is shredded coconut and your creativity. Shredded coconut comes in many textures and sizes: fine, medium, and large. You will also need juice or pulp from fruits and vegetables to create your desired colors. Add superfood powders or colored tea, if you like. You can create any shades you want.

I divide shredded coconut into several small bowls. I add just a bit of coloring ingredients and mix well. Make sure you have a separate spoon for each color. Use the following pigments for your desired color:

- **Yellow:** turmeric powder or saffron
- **Red:** beet, raspberry, or cherry juice
- **Pink:** cactus fruit or pomegranate
- **Purple:** plums, grapes, or purple cabbage juice
- **Blue:** Thai tea or Blue Majik powder by E3 Live
- **Green:** spinach juice, matcha green tea, spirulina, or moringa powder

Mix coconut shreds with the pigment of your choice, and let them absorb the color. If you add lemon or lime juice, your color will change.

You can serve the coconut wet like this, or dry out in a dehydrator at 110°F. If you don't have a dehydrator, use the lowest setting of your oven, around 200°F. If you do use the oven, watch the coconut closely so it won't burn, as it turns brown very quickly.

Store the sprinkles in small glass jars or plastic containers. Use them for decorating your food art masterpieces. Note that quantities depend on how much you need, but I use approximately 1 tablespoon of coconut shreds per 1 teaspoon of juice, or more if you want a stronger color. Colors will vary depending on the natural pigments you use.

You can also use lemon zest, rose petals, or crushed pistachios as your sprinkles.

GARBANZO-BEAN BUCKWHEAT BANANA BREAD (gluten-free)

Serves 8-10

2 cups garbanzo bean flour
1 cup buckwheat flour
1 cup water
5 large ripe bananas, mashed
3-4 tablespoons date sugar, or more if you want sweeter bread
1 teaspoon baking powder
1 teaspoon coconut oil, plus more for greasing pan
1 teaspoon Ceylon cinnamon
1/2 teaspoon baking soda

DIRECTIONS:

1. Preheat oven to 350°F.
2. Mix all ingredients in a large mixing bowl.
3. Grease a loaf pan with coconut oil and fold in the mixture. You can add walnuts and/or almonds on top.
4. Bake for 50-60 minutes. Serve with sliced fruits.

VARIATION: You can use this recipe to make muffins. Bake for about 45 minutes, or until ready. You can add vegan chocolate chips, almonds, walnuts, and raisins to this recipe.

COCONUT WHIPPED CREAM (gluten-free)

1-2 (15-ounce) cans full-fat coconut milk
1-2 tablespoons vanilla extract
sweetener to taste: maple syrup, coconut sugar, or raw coconut nectar

DIRECTIONS:

1. Refrigerate the coconut milk overnight.
2. Don't shake the can. Gently scoop out the coconut cream from the top, making sure that you do not take any liquid (you may save the coconut water for another recipe, such as a smoothie, soup, or stew).
3. With a hand mixer or stand mixer, start whipping the coconut cream. Beat for 5 to 10 minutes or until smooth. If liquid starts to separate from the coconut cream, drain it off.
4. Add vanilla extract and sweetener and beat until the mixture reaches the consistency of whipped cream.
5. Use immediately or store in a glass container in refrigerator for up to 2 days.

CASHEW BUTTERCREAM FROSTING (raw/gluten-free)

This frosting can be used over muffins, cakes, iced coffee, ice cream, etc.

2 cups raw unsalted cashews, soaked for 4 hours
1/2 cup coconut oil, melted
1/3 cup maple syrup
1/3 cup water or coconut water
1 tablespoon vanilla extract
1/2 teaspoon almond extract
1/2 teaspoon raw apple cider vinegar
1/8 teaspoon Celtic salt

DIRECTIONS:

1. Drain and rinse cashews. Place in a high-speed blender or food processor along with remaining ingredients. Blend on high until smooth and creamy.
2. Transfer frosting to a shallow bowl and freeze for 30 minutes.
3. Take frosting out of the freezer and whip with a hand blender until fluffy and light. If the mixture is not cold enough, it won't whip up, so you may have to continue to freeze it in between blending.
4. Cover and refrigerate for up to 1 week.

VARIATION: Create different frosting flavors by adding lemon zest or lemon juice for lemon flavor, 1 tablespoon raw cacao powder or carob powder for chocolate, 1-2 tablespoons matcha green tea powder for green tea flavor, or 1/2 teaspoon rose or orange blossom water for exotic flavor.

Make Double or You Will Be in Trouble Peruvian Bread Pudding

by Mayra Sollazzo (Peru)

Mayra Sollazzo was born in Peru. She immigrated to the United States as a teenager but kept her Peruvian traditions and customs. Mayra is a dual-language school teacher, a happy wife, and mom of three little girls and a dog. She is also a volleyball player and a great belly dancer. Every day, she uses healthy recipes to cook homemade meals for her family. For Mayra, traditional Peruvian food brings great memories of her grandmother, Mama Alicia, and their cooking together. Her recipe for Peruvian Bread Pudding is very popular and loved by many. The following is a veganized version by Aleksandra and Mayra, approved by the whole family.

Serves 8–10

Coconut Caramel:

1 1/2 cups raw coconut sugar
1/2 cup unsweetened coconut milk
1/2 tablespoon coconut oil, melted
1 tablespoon vanilla extract
1/2 tablespoon pure vanilla powder

Pudding:

2 1/2 cups unsweetened coconut milk
3 tablespoons chia seeds
2 tablespoons flaxseed meal
1 cup walnuts, chopped
1 cup raisins
1 1/2 pounds/24 ounces/680 grams organic sliced multigrain bread or whole-wheat bread (I used the one from Trader Joe's)
2 tablespoons vanilla Bourbon extract
1/4 cup maple syrup
Bourbon, for serving

DIRECTIONS:

1. In a heavy skillet over very low heat, melt all ingredients. Let caramelize for 10–20 minutes. Keep stirring it so the mixture won't burn.
2. Quickly pour into medium-size Pyrex dish or a glass pie dish. Allow to cool for about 10 minutes. Make the pudding:
3. Preheat oven to 350°F.
4. Mix milk, chia seeds, and flaxseed meal in a small bowl. Let soak for 10–15 minutes.
5. In a large mixing bowl, combine the walnuts and raisins. Tear the bread into not-too-long pieces and add to the bowl. Add the milk with chia and flax along with vanilla and maple syrup. Combine well with your clean hands or a mixing spoon.
6. Transfer the pudding to the dish with the caramel. Smooth it on top of the caramel and bake for 45 minutes.
7. Serve warm with **You May Be Surprised, But This Ice Cream Tastes So Nice (see recipe page 131)** and 1–3 drops of Bourbon, or place in a refrigerator and serve cold. Cut into small pieces, about 3 inches long.

TO DIE FOR CARROT CAKE
by Leah Pozsgay
(inspired by Hungarian baking)
(gluten-free)

Leah Pozsgay, a New York City resident, is a longtime nutrition enthusiast but decided at the end of 2016 that she was going to leave her fifteen-plus-year career on Wall Street to align her heart with her true passion of health and wellness. Leah enrolled in the Institute for Integrative Nutrition (IIN) and will become a certified health coach in September 2017. She is fully immersed in school but now has more time for other passions, such as yoga, healthy cooking, and traveling. She will be enrolling in YogaWorks 200-hour yoga teacher training in the fall and hopes to bring healthy eating, holistic healing, and a yoga practice to her future clients.

To make this cake, combine the first five ingredients and set them aside for at least twenty minutes or refrigerate overnight. Follow the rest of the recipe the next day.

Serves 8
Cake:
1 cup finely grated carrots (choose the finest side of the grater)
1/2 cup applesauce
1/3 cup melted coconut oil (replace with more applesauce if you don't mind the gummy texture)
2 teaspoons apple cider vinegar
2 teaspoons pure vanilla extract
1 1/2 cups oat flour
1/2 cup maple syrup, or
more if you like a sweeter taste
1/2 cup finely shredded coconut, chopped walnuts, or raisins (optional)
1 teaspoon cinnamon
3/4 teaspoon salt
1/2 teaspoon baking soda

Icing:
1 cup **Cashew Buttercream Frosting (see recipe page 151)**

DIRECTIONS:
1. Whisk the first five ingredients together and let sit for at least twenty minutes or marinate overnight in a refrigerator before moving on to the rest of the instructions.
2. Preheat oven to 350°F. Line an 8-inch square pan with parchment paper or grease well.
3. In a separate bowl, mix together all the remaining ingredients. Pour marinated wet ingredients into dry ingredients, and then stir until just combined; don't overmix.
4. Pour batter into the prepared pan and smooth down evenly. Bake for 30–40 minutes or until toothpick inserted in cake comes out clean.
5. Let cool and spread cashew frosting over the cake.

VARIATION: This recipe works with spelt flour as well or use the batter to make cupcakes instead of a single cake.

HIGH PROTEIN CHOCOLATE ENERGY BARS
by Vera Wanga Daut
(raw/gluten-free)

Vera Wanga Daut is a health, fitness, and life coach. She was inspired to become vegan by Olenko's beautiful recipes and passion for healthy eating. After she accepted and completed a ten-day vegan challenge, Vera felt great and decided to transition to a plant-based diet.

Giving up meat and animal products provided her with numerous benefits: she lost weight, she sleeps better, and she feels better overall. Now that she is a vegan, people ask her what she eats and where she gets her protein from. That's why she created this recipe for High Protein Chocolate Energy Bars.
www.verawangadaut.wordpress.com

Serves 12
2 scoops vegan chocolate protein shake powder
1 cup quick-cooking old-fashioned rolled oats

1/2 cup raw walnuts, chopped
1/2 cup dates, chopped
1 teaspoon sunflower seeds
1 teaspoon chia seeds
1/2 cup unsweetened almond milk
1/4 cup all natural creamy peanut butter
2 teaspoons maple syrup

DIRECTIONS:

1. Combine protein shake, oats, walnuts, dates, and seeds in a large mixing bowl. Mix well.
2. Add remaining ingredients and mix well.
3. Press mixture into 7x5-inch baking pan. Cover and refrigerate for at least 3 hours.
4. Cut into twelve bars.

German Chocolate Cake Milkshake

by Ashley Diana
(inspired by German baking)
(raw/gluten-free)

Ashley Diana is a Las Vegas resident, a healthy lifestyle expert, and a beauty professional. She received a Plant-Based Nutrition Certification from Dr. T. Campbell at Cornell University. Being a self-taught plant-based chef, she creates nutritious recipes to share with her supporters each week through her blog and social media. In addition to recipes, she writes about cruelty-free beauty and healthy lifestyle products. A new mom, Ashley also promotes healthy baby products. Look for Ashley's healthy shake recipes in her e-book, Marvelous Milkshakes. www.ashleydiana.com

Serves 1-2
1 cup non-dairy milk
1/4 cup pecans
2 ripe frozen bananas
3 Medjool dates, pitted
3 tablespoons shredded coconut
2 tablespoons cocoa powder
1/4 teaspoon pure vanilla extract

DIRECTIONS: Process all ingredients in a high-speed blender.

Photo: Ashley Diana

CHAPTER 14

Peas to the World with Happy Veggies for Dinner

RAINBOW PIZZA

Serves 2

Dough:
3 1/2–4 cups bread flour
1 envelope instant dry yeast
2 teaspoons salt
1 teaspoon sugar
1 1/2 cups water at 110°F
2 tablespoons plus 2 teaspoons olive oil

Sauce and cheese:
Mushroom Marinara (see recipe page 160)
Not Your Mom's Mozzarella Cheese (see recipe page 87)

Toppings:
cherry tomatoes, sun-dried tomatoes, bell pepper, green peas, cooked purple potatoes, cooked carrots, cooked yams, corn, onion

DIRECTIONS:

1. Make dough: Combine the bread flour, yeast, salt, and sugar in a bowl of a stand-mixer and process. (If you don't have a stand-mixer, mix it by hand.)
2. While the mixer is running, slowly add the water and 2 tablespoons oil. Mix until the dough forms a ball. If dough is sticky, add more flour, 1 tablespoon at a time, until it becomes a solid ball. If dough is too dry, add more water, 1 tablespoon at a time.
3. Scrape the dough onto a lightly floured surface and knead into a firm ball.
4. Grease a large bowl with the remaining 2 teaspoons olive oil and add the dough. Cover the bowl with a kitchen towel and place in a warm area for about an hour to let it double in size.
5. Turn the dough out onto a lightly floured surface and divide into two equal parts. Cover each with a kitchen towel and let rest for about 10 minutes.
6. Use a rolling pin or your hands to stretch the dough gradually into a desired shape, such as a circle or heart.
7. Finish pizza: Preheat oven to 400°F.
8. Spread sauce evenly over crust and top with mozzarella cheese.
9. Arrange chosen vegetables on top to form a rainbow.
10. Bake for 30 minutes or until ready.

VARIATIONS: Bread flour will give you a crispy crust. Use all-purpose flour for a chewier crust. You can also make a crust with butternut squash, zucchini, or eggplant.

Lentil Meatballs
Family Style

(gluten-free)

Serves 45-50

2 cups sun-dried tomatoes, soaked

a few parsley sprigs

1 bunch basil

2 sweet potatoes, cooked

4 cups lentils, cooked

1 small onion, chopped

4 cloves garlic

juice of 1/2 lemon

1 cup teff, cooked

4 tablespoons flax seeds

4 tablespoons pumpkin seeds

1/2 teaspoon paprika

1/2 teaspoon curry

1 teaspoon pink Himalayan salt

Mushroom Marinara (see recipe page 160)

DIRECTIONS:

1. Preheat oven to 350°F.

2. In a food processor, combine sun-dried tomatoes, parsley, and basil and pulse.

3. Peel sweet potatoes and add to food processor along with the lentils. Pulse until smooth.

4. Transfer mixture to a big bowl. Add onion, garlic, lemon juice, teff, flax seeds, pumpkin seeds, paprika, curry, and salt. Mix well.

5. With clean hands, form mixture into meatballs. Place on a baking sheet and bake in oven for about 30-40 minutes.

6. Place baked meatballs in a casserole dish. Pour sauce over and place back in oven for additional 5–10 minutes.

Mushroom Marinara
by Paul E Calarco Jr. (Italy)
(gluten-free)

Dr. Paul E Calarco Jr. is a mindful professor of sociology, professional disc jockey, and father of two beautiful boys. Among his diverse global epicurean interests has been the drive and search to seamlessly integrate vegan alternatives into traditional dishes. He desires a future where the access to these products and solutions are mainstream staples rather than an exotic expedition.

5 tablespoons extra virgin olive oil
1 medium Vidalia onion, chopped
2–4 garlic cloves, minced
4 fresh Roma tomatoes, coarsely chopped
1 (8-ounce) package baby Bella mushrooms, chopped
1/2 teaspoon pink Himalayan salt, plus more to taste
1 (14-ounce) can crushed tomatoes
1 (14-ounce) can diced tomatoes
1 (8-ounce) can tomato sauce
2 teaspoons parsley
1 teaspoon oregano
1/2 teaspoon basil
2 dried bay leaves

DIRECTIONS:
1. In a large pot, heat the oil over medium-high heat. Add the onion and garlic and sauté for about 5 minutes. Be careful not to scald garlic.
2. Add Roma tomatoes, mushrooms, and salt and sauté for another 5 minutes.
3. Add remaining ingredients along with about 8 ounces water (I use the water to rinse the cans out so as not to waste any tomato sauce) and bring to slight boil. Turn down the heat and simmer with cover partially open on low heat 40–50 minutes, stirring every 10 minutes.
5. Season with additional salt to taste.

MOROCCAN VEGETABLE TAGINE
by Executive Chef Azzeddine Bennouna (Morocco) (gluten-free)

Azzeddine Bennouna was born and raised in Morocco. He opened his first travel agency, Le Soleil Tours, in 1984 and started organizing tours to Morocco and France until September 2011. He opened his first restaurant in the New York's meatpacking district in 1996 and followed it by opening his second restaurant for Moroccan cuisine, Zitoune, in Mamaroneck, New York, in 2007, and then Olivia Wine Bar and Mediterranean Tapas in New York's East Village. Presently, Azzeddine has returned to his native country to run his tour company, Cynab Voyages, which he opened in 1997. He also offers cooking classes at his home. www.cynabvoyages.com

Serves 4
4 cloves garlic, crushed
1/2 pound flat-leaf (Italian) parsley, coarsely chopped
1/2 pound cilantro, coarsely chopped
4 tablespoons olive oil
2 carrots, cut into halves or thirds
4 small potatoes, peeled
2 tomatoes, peeled and cut into quarters
2 parsnips, cut into halves or thirds
2 turnips, cut into halves or thirds

2 zucchini, cut into halves or thirds (or 4 whole small ones)
1 whole green pepper
1 teaspoon paprika
1 teaspoon ground cumin
20 whole green olives
preserved lemon (optional)
salt and pepper to taste

DIRECTIONS:
1. In a large pan, slowly cook the garlic, parsley, and cilantro in the olive oil. Add carrots and cook until they start softening.
2. Add potatoes. Cook for a few minutes, and then add the remaining vegetables.
3. Add paprika and cumin to taste. Cover the pan and cook for about 30 minutes.
4. Add olives and preserved lemon. Taste and adjust salt and pepper as necessary. Serve hot.

THAI NOODLES WITH ORANGE LENTIL
(gluten-free)

Serves 2
3 ramen cakes (forbidden rice or another flavor) or clear rice noodles
2 cups orange lentils, cooked
1 large heirloom tomato
1 piece pimento
1/2 cup peanut butter or almond butter
3 tablespoons Bragg liquid aminos or coconut aminos
3 tablespoons raw apple cider vinegar
1 tablespoon red onion, chopped
1/3 teaspoon pink Himalayan salt

1/2 teaspoon curry powder
1/8 teaspoon cayenne pepper or more to taste
1 tablespoon scallions, chopped
juice of 1/2 lime
fresh mint
fresh basil

DIRECTIONS:
1. Prepare ramen cakes according to the instructions on the package.
2. Combine remaining ingredients in a big bowl and mix gently. Add water if too thick.
3. Add ramen cakes and stir. Enjoy!

NO-NOODLE LASAGNA
(gluten-free)

By replacing lasagna noodles with thinly sliced zucchini, you create a delicious, low-carb, and gluten-free dish that your family will love. You can make this ahead of time and bring to a family gathering, picnic, or BBQ—or even freeze for later.

Serves 6–8
4 zucchini
Mushroom Marinara Sauce (see recipe page 160)
Macadamia Nut Ricotta Cheese (see recipe page 87)

DIRECTIONS:
1. Preheat oven to 350°F.
2. Slice zucchini lengthwise into thin strips (use a mandolin or a knife).
3. Line bottom of a deep 7x11-inch lasagna dish with zucchini strips.
4. Ladle marinara sauce on top of the zucchini and spread.
5. Layer ricotta cheese.
6. Repeat steps 3–5 two more times.
7. Ladle marinara sauce on top.
8. Bake the lasagna for 30–40 minutes.

VARIATIONS: Add additional vegetables like spinach, peppers, eggplant, mushrooms, etc. Sprinkle nutritional yeast and oregano flakes with the ricotta layer.

Rainbow Sushi

(gluten-free)

Serves 2-4

15 ounces rice of your choice, cooked
(I like to use Lotus Foods)
2 sweet potatoes, cooked
2 purple potatoes, cooked
1/2 teaspoon spirulina powder
1/2 teaspoon Blue Majik powder
1/2–1 teaspoon beet powder
1/2 teaspoon turmeric
1 teaspoon lemon juice
nori seaweed sheets
1 cucumber
a few asparagus spears
1 avocado
baby tomatoes, for serving

DIRECTIONS:

1. Cook rice following instructions on package. Let cool and divide into 4 serving bowls.
2. Cook potatoes in another pot. Let cool and then peel.
3. Place sweet potatoes and purple potatoes in two separate serving bowls and mash with a fork.
4. Add coloring ingredients to the rice bowls: spirulina powder for green, Blue Majik powder for blue, beet powder for red, and turmeric for yellow.
5. Divide purple potatoes into two parts. Add lemon juice to one part to obtain a hot pink color.
6. Place a sushi mat on a cutting board and center a nori sheet on it. Spread different rice colors thinly on the nori. Cut the cucumber, asparagus, and avocado into thin strips and arrange on the nori sheet. Lift the end of the mat and gently roll over the ingredients. Cut into sushi slices.
7. Serve with baby tomatoes on the side.

VARIATIONS: Use quinoa in place of the rice.
 • Add apple cider vinegar to some rice bowls for a variety of flavor.
 • Serve with your favorite sauce.
 • Use different vegetables: bell peppers, mushrooms, carrots, radishes, beets, sun-dried tomatoes, butternut squash, edamame, roasted eggplant, artichoke, raw cheese, tofu, etc.

ZUCCHINI PASTA WITH BLUEBERRY SAUCE
(gluten-free)

Serves 2-4

Pasta:

3–4 medium zucchini

Sauce:

2 cups wild blueberries, fresh or frozen

2 ripe, frozen bananas

4 Medjool dates, pitted

1/2 cup cashews or coconut butter

3 tablespoons coconut water or filtered water

1 cup fresh or frozen blueberries

fresh basil

DIRECTIONS:

1. Run zucchini through a spiral pasta maker, such as Spirooli.

2. Combine all sauce ingredients in a high-speed blender. Serve over zucchini pasta.

3. Garnish with blueberries and basil.

VARIATIONS: If you want your sauce to be sweeter, add more dates. You may serve it with cooked pasta if you prefer. The riper the bananas, the sweeter the sauce will be.

 • Wild blueberries have a high amount of antioxidants. If you are using frozen blueberries, thaw them first, and you may use more water.

 • Use this sauce over steel oats, quinoa, or rice for a quick meal or as a dessert.

SUPER QUICK MUSHROOM STEW
(gluten-free)

Serves 1-2

1 small onion, chopped

2–3 cloves garlic

1 sweet potato, cubed

4–5 lime leaves

4 1/3 ounces enoki mushrooms, sliced

5 1/3 ounces shiitake mushrooms (or any other kind), sliced

1 teaspoon curry

1/2 teaspoon ginger

1 bunch scallions

12 ounces firm tofu
1 can coconut milk
pink Himalayan salt, to taste
Steaming Quinoa (recipe follows)

DIRECTIONS:

1. Place onion and garlic in a pot. Cover with 1 cup water. Sauté for a few minutes until tender (I don't use oil to cook).
2. Add sweet potato, lime leaves, and mushrooms and continue sautéing.
3. When vegetables are tender, add curry, ginger, and scallions. Cut tofu into cubes and add to the pot.
4. Pour in coconut milk at the end of cooking for a creamy texture.
5. Season with salt on your plate. Serve with quinoa.

VARIATION: For this stew, you may use any vegetables at hand, such as spinach, zucchini, kale, cauliflower, broccoli, etc.

STEAMING QUINOA
(gluten-free)

Serves 1-2
1 cup quinoa

DIRECTIONS:

1. Rinse quinoa well to get rid of the soapy taste.
2. Combine quinoa and 2 cups pure water in a pot. Cover and cook for about 10 minutes.
3. Turn off the heat and let sit for another 5 minutes or until the water is completely absorbed.

VARIATIONS: The quinoa may be used as a savory dish or a sweet one for breakfast and dessert.

OKRA WITH RICE
by Carol-Ann Cook (Inspired by Southern Cuisine) (gluten-free)

Carol-Ann Cook is an embryology technologist, helping couples conceive. She works full-time in a busy IVF program in New York City. After commuting three hours total every day, she needs to be able to prepare quick and healthy meals when she finally arrives home.

Serves 2-4
2 teaspoons olive or coconut oil
1/4 teaspoon sweet onion or shallot, finely chopped
8 ounces fresh or frozen okra, cut into 1/4-inch rounds
1 plum tomato, chopped
sweetener, such as stevia, maple syrup, or agave (optional)
salt and pepper to taste
2 cups cooked brown, wild, or basmati rice

DIRECTIONS:

1. Heat oil in a skillet or wok. Add onion and sauté until translucent.
2. Add okra and sauté until softened.
3. Add tomato and sauté until softened. You may want to add a little sweetener to take away some of the acidity of the tomato, if necessary.
4. Remove from heat, season with salt and pepper to taste, and serve over cooked rice.

The Burger She Wrote
(gluten-free)

Serves 12-15, depending on size

2 1/4 cups lentils, cooked

2 cups quinoa, cooked

1 1/2 cups sweet potato, cooked (you can keep the skin on if organic)

1 cup sun-dried tomatoes, soaked

1 onion

1 bunch parsley or cilantro

2 cloves garlic, chopped

juice of 1/2 lemon

3 tablespoons sunflower seeds

3 tablespoons pumpkin seeds

2 tablespoons flax seeds

1 teaspoon pink Himalayan salt, or more

1/3 teaspoon smoked paprika

DIRECTIONS:

1. Preheat oven to 350°F.
2. Pulse lentils, quinoa, sweet potato, sun-dried tomatoes, onion, and parsley in a food processor.
3. Transfer mixture to a big bowl and add remaining ingredients. Mix by hand.
4. Scoop mixture and form burgers. Place burgers on a baking sheet.
5. Bake burgers for about 30 minutes. Flip over and bake for another 10 minutes or more.
6. Serve with rolls or over salads. Keep in the fridge for a few days or freeze them for later.

VARIATIONS: Instead of sweet potatoes, use pumpkin or butternut squash.

- Instead of lentils, use beans.
- Add walnuts or pecans.

Mixed Vegetables

by Jenna Davila (gluten-free)

Jenna Davila is a plant-based health/wellness coach, spiritual counselor, high-raw vegan food blogger, and freelance photographer. Her mission is to illuminate the vitality of living plant-based food and share her experience to help others find authentic energetic balance and emotional, physical, and mental health. Her passion is spreading the message of veganism and protecting and loving all living beings on the planet. Jenna loves experimenting in the kitchen and coming up with unique meals and smoothies that show how diverse and delicious this lifestyle can be.
www.livepureblog.com

Serves 1-2
2 cups Brussels sprouts, halved
1/2 red onion, diced
3 garlic cloves, minced
1 red bell pepper, cut into 1-inch strips
2 cups spaghetti squash, cooked
1–2 very large handfuls mixed greens
1 handful pecans, chopped
Sweet and Smoky Tahini Mustard (recipe follows on a side)

DIRECTIONS:
1. Place Brussels sprouts, red onion, and garlic in a bamboo steamer and steam for 10 minutes.
2. Add red bell pepper and steam for 5 minutes. Transfer all steamed ingredients to a large mixing bowl along with the spaghetti squash.
3. Add a tablespoon of the Sweet and Smoky Tahini Mustard into the mixing bowl, and use tongs to mix it together with the vegetables. Add more sauce as you desire.
4. Add mixed greens, mix with the sauced vegetables, and garnish with pecans. Serve with **Sweet and Smoky Tahini Mustard**

SWEET AND SMOKY TAHINI MUSTARD
by Jenna (raw/gluten-free)

2 tablespoons tahini
2 tablespoons filtered water
1 tablespoon Dijon mustard,
1 tablespoon sweetener: date syrup, maple syrup, or 1–2 Medjool dates
1 tablespoon lemon juice
3/4 teaspoon smoked paprika

DIRECTIONS: Blend all ingredients together and set aside. Serve with Mixed Vegetables.

BIBIMBAP
by Sarah Kim (gluten-free)

Sarah Kim was born and raised in South Korea and immigrated to the United States many years ago. She is an elementary school teacher and is studying to become an acupuncturist. She is fascinated by traditional healing practices and medicine, especially herbs and acupuncture. She loves cooking healthy Korean food for her family and friends and introducing people to Asian vegetables and fruits. This recipe is for a dish that is popular in Korea.

Serves 4
3 cups short-grain rice

Gosari:
2 cups boiled gosari (fernbrake), optional
1 teaspoon sesame oil
1 teaspoon minced garlic
1/2 teaspoon sesame seeds
pinch pepper
1 teaspoon vegetable oil

Soybean sprouts:
16 ounces soybean sprouts
1 teaspoon minced garlic
2 teaspoons sesame oil
1/2 teaspoon sesame seeds
salt and pepper to taste

Spinach:
1 bunch spinach
1 teaspoon chopped scallion
1 teaspoon minced garlic
1 teaspoon sesame oil
1/2 teaspoon sesame seeds
salt and pepper to taste.

Shiitake mushrooms:
3 shiitake mushrooms
vegetable oil
1/4 teaspoon salt

Zucchini:
1 small zucchini
salt
1 teaspoon chopped scallion
1/2 teaspoon minced garlic
1 teaspoon sesame oil
1/2 teaspoon sesame seeds
oil, for sautéing

Carrots:
1 medium carrot
oil, for sautéing
salt and pepper to taste

Hot sauce:
4 tablespoons Korean red chili pepper paste (gochujang)
1 teaspoon sugar
1 teaspoon sesame oil
3 teaspoons water
sesame oil, for serving

DIRECTIONS:

1. Prepare the rice: Cook rice in a rice cooker, using a little less water than called for. The rice for bibimbap should be a little drier than usual.

2. Prepare gosari: Cut gosari into 3-inch strips. Season with soy sauce, sesame oil, garlic, sesame seeds, and pepper. Let stand for 10 minutes. Heat vegetable oil in a skillet over medium heat. Add gosari and sauté for about 5 minutes over medium heat.

3. Prepare soybean sprouts: Bring 3 cups salted water to a boil. Add sprouts and boil for 5 minutes. Drain quickly and shock in cold water. Drain again. Toss with garlic, sesame oil, sesame seeds, salt, and pepper.

4. Prepare spinach: Put spinach in boiling salted

water for 40 seconds. Drain quickly and shock in cold water. Drain again. Toss with scallion, garlic, sesame oil, sesame seeds, salt, and pepper.

5. Prepare shiitake mushrooms: Clean and rinse mushrooms, then thinly slice. Place in a wok with vegetable oil and salt. Cook until done, approximately 3 minutes.

6. Prepare zucchini: Halve zucchini lengthwise, and then thinly slice crosswise. Generously sprinkle salt over sliced zucchini and set aside for 10–15 minutes. Squeeze out excess liquid from salted zucchini by hand. Add scallion, garlic, sesame oil, and sesame seeds. Sauté in a lightly oiled skillet for 1–2 minutes over medium-high heat.

7. Prepare carrots: Cut carrots into 2-inch pieces and slice thinly. Sauté in a lightly oiled skillet for 3 minutes over medium-high heat, sprinkling on salt and pepper to taste.

8. Prepare hot sauce: In a small bowl, combine all ingredients and mix well.

9. To assemble: Place a serving of rice into a big bowl. Nicely add a small amount of each prepared vegetable. Drizzle a little sesame oil over, and place 2 or 3 teaspoons of hot sauce in the middle. Mix all the ingredients and the vegetables with the hot sauce. Serve and enjoy.

INNER PEAS WITH CHEESY QUINOA (gluten-free)

Serves 2-4
16 ounces frozen peas, thawed
3 cups quinoa, cooked
1 cup **Not Your Mom's Mozzarella (see recipe page 87)**
salt to taste
Olenko's Kitchen Revolution Toasted Cumin Spice Mix (see recipe page 105)

DIRECTIONS: Combine all ingredients in a big bowl. Season with salt and spice mix.

Sweet Potato Quiche
(gluten-free)

Serves 4-6

Crust:
2 medium to large sweet potatoes

Filling:
1 onion, chopped into small pieces
1 small crown broccoli, chopped into small pieces
1 (6-ounce) bag baby spinach
15 1/2 ounces tofu
3 flaxseed eggs
2 cloves garlic, chopped
2 tablespoons liquid aminos
1/2 teaspoon curry powder
1 teaspoon salt
pepper
1 cup **Not Your Mom's Mozzarella (see recipe page 87)** or **Cashew Sour Cream (see recipe page 90)**, for topping
1 tablespoon nutritional yeast
3 tablespoons fresh parsley, chopped

VARIATIONS: You can add other veggies, such as mushrooms, peppers, tomatoes, olives, leeks, etc. Just experiment.

DIRECTIONS:

1. Preheat oven to 400°F.
2. Make the crust: Peel sweet potatoes and slice on a mandolin. (If you don't have a mandolin, slice them with a knife as thinly as possible.)
3. In a glass pie dish, lay the sweet potato slices out in a circular pattern. Overlap the pieces so that when they bake and shrink a little, they are still overlapping. You may not use all of the potato.
4. Bake the sweet potato "crust" for 15 minutes. Remove from the oven and lower heat to 350°F.
5. Make the filling: Put onion and broccoli in a pot with 1 cup water. Add spinach and boil for 2–3 minutes. Turn off the stove.
6. In a large bowl, combine tofu, flaxseed eggs, garlic, liquid aminos, curry powder, nutritional yeast, parsley, salt, and pepper. Mash with a potato masher. (You can use a food processor if you prefer.)
7. Add the onion, broccoli, and spinach without the broth. (You can use the broth for a soup base later.) Stir the mixture, and if the veggies are too big, chop them into smaller pieces.
8. Pour the veggie mixture onto the sweet-potato crust and smooth out to ensure the filling is evenly distributed.
9. Bake for 10 minutes, and then top with nut cheese. Bake for another 10–20 minutes, or until ready.
10. Serve with salad on the side.

Cauliflower Fried Rice

by Rachael Paquett (gluten-free)

Rachel Paquett, my cousin, is a mom of two boys. She loves running, lifting weights, yoga, cooking, and baking healthy for her family. Her older son is always in the kitchen with her wanting to "help." It's important that the ingredients she uses are nutrient-rich and healthy, but they have to taste good, too.

Serves 2-4
1 onion
4–5 cloves garlic
coconut oil
1-inch fresh ginger
1 cauliflower
4 carrots
sesame oil
coconut aminos
1 cup peas

DIRECTIONS:
1. Sauté onion and garlic with coconut oil until fragrant. Add ginger and sauté a little more.
2. Pulse cauliflower in a high-speed blender until it has a rice-like consistency.
3. Peel and pulse carrots (or dice if you prefer).
4. Add carrots to the pan. Sauté, and then add cauliflower. Drizzle in sesame oil.
5. Add coconut aminos to taste. Lastly, add peas. Mix and cook on low until cauliflower browns.

EVERYTHING FROM THE GARDEN SPAGHETTI SQUASH
by Diana Sinnott (gluten-free)

Diana Sinnott, my cousin, is an eighth-grade math teacher. She enjoys cooking and baking in her free time and teaches a cooking class at a local camp in the summer. When she is not working (or in the kitchen), she enjoys being outside or traveling with her husband, Bobby.

Serves 2-4
1 large spaghetti squash
2 tablespoons extra virgin olive oil, more if needed
2 cloves garlic, minced
1 small onion, diced
1 green pepper, sliced
1 red bell pepper, sliced
1/2 cup eggplant, medium diced
1 cup mushrooms, sliced
1/4 cup Kalamata olives, halved
1 cup cherry tomatoes, halved
salt and pepper to taste
parsley, chopped

DIRECTIONS:
1. Preheat oven to 450°F.
2. Halve squash lengthwise. Use a spoon to scoop out and discard seeds from the middle of each half.
3. Arrange squash in a 9x13-inch casserole dish, cut-side down. Add enough water to the dish to surround the sides of the squash about 1/2-inch deep. Bake until just tender, about 45 to 55 minutes. Remove from the oven, drain, and let rest until cool enough to handle.
4. While the squash is cooling, heat 2 tablespoons extra virgin olive oil in a large pan over medium heat. Add garlic, onion, peppers, and eggplant. Cook for 3–4 minutes or until peppers and eggplant are tender.
5. Add mushrooms, olives, and tomatoes, and heat 2–3 minutes.
6. Rake a fork back and forth across the squash to remove its flesh in strands. Add squash to pan of vegetables to combine. Add more olive oil if necessary and season with salt and pepper. Garnish with parsley.

CHICKPEA AND CAULIFLOWER WITH QUINOA
by Sunny Gandara (gluten-free)

Sunny Gandara is a professionally trained chef through the Institute for Culinary Education. She owned her own catering company in the Hudson Valley of New York for five years. She holds the plant-based certificate from Cornell and today works as a Life Design Coach with an emphasis on the benefits of a vegan lifestyle. www.sunnygandara.com

Serves 2-4
1 large head cauliflower, cut into florets
4 tablespoons olive oil, divided
2 cloves garlic, smashed
1 teaspoon toasted **Ras el Hanout (see recipe page 106)**
1 1/2 cups organic chickpeas, cooked
1/2 teaspoon kosher salt
1/4 teaspoon freshly ground black pepper
1 cup plain vegan yogurt
1/2 cup tahini
1/2 cup water or less
1 tablespoon tamari
1 clove garlic, minced
1 cup quinoa, cooked
juice and zest of 1 lemon
1/2 cup fresh flat-leaf parsley, chopped
1/4 cup pine nuts, toasted

DIRECTIONS:
1. Preheat oven to 400°F.
2. Combine cauliflower and 2 tablespoons of the oil and toss. Bake for 20 minutes or until cauliflower is tender, lightly roasted, and browned.
3. Place remaining 2 tablespoons oil in a large pot over medium heat. Add garlic and sauté until lightly caramelized and fragrant. Add Ras el Hanout and sauté until flavors are fragrant.
4. Add chickpeas and mix well. Season with salt and pepper.
5. Combine yogurt, tahini, water, tamari, and garlic in a high-speed blender and blend until emulsified. Season dressing with salt and pepper. Reserve.
6. Combine cauliflower, quinoa, and chickpea mixture in a large mixing bowl and mix well. Season with parsley, fresh lemon juice, and lemon zest. Add pine nuts and drizzle dressing over.

BLACK BEANS WITH QUINOA
by Christine Miskinis (Inspired by Puerto Rican Cuisine) (gluten-free)

Christine is a women's empowerment coach who focuses on teaching women how to tune in to their inner voice to express their authentic voice in their lives. She is the owner and founder of Rock it Out, Woman, which began with healing her own voice when she found out at age twenty-four that she had pre-cancerous cells growing from her stomach up into her esophagus from a lifetime of digestive issues. Christine has started a movement called Rock Your VOICE, Woman, to ignite the voices of women entrepreneurs and create social change in our world. www.rockitoutwoman.com

Serves 2-4
1 tablespoon organic olive oil
4 organic garlic cloves, finely chopped
1 organic yellow onion
3/4 cup organic quinoa
1 1/2 cups vegetable broth
1 teaspoon cumin
dash cayenne powder
1 teaspoon salt
pepper to taste
1/2 cup frozen organic corn kernels
1/2 cup frozen organic peas
29 ounces organic black beans
1/2 cup cilantro, finely chopped

DIRECTIONS:
1. Heat large pan over medium heat for 1–2 minutes and add olive oil.
2. Add garlic and onion and sauté until slightly browned.
3. Add quinoa and broth and mix thoroughly.
4. Add cumin, cayenne, salt, and pepper. Allow the mixture to begin to boil.
5. Cover with a lid, and simmer on very low heat for 20 minutes until quinoa is soft and fluffy.
6. Stir in corn, peas, beans, and cilantro. Cover with a lid, and simmer for another 3–5 minutes until everything is warm.

Butternut Squash and Eggplant Pizza Lovers' Pizzas

(gluten-free)

Serves 6-8

1 medium butternut squash

1 large eggplant

Not Your Mom's Mozzarella Cheese (see page 87)

rainbow veggies (cooked sweet potatoes, bell peppers, cherry tomatoes, mushrooms, onion, corn, etc.)

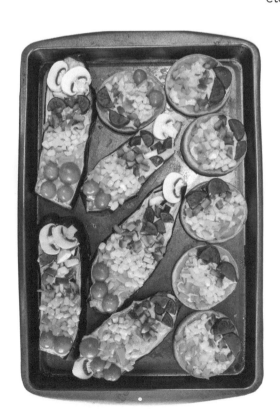

DIRECTIONS:

1. Preheat oven to 350°F.
2. Slice the slim end of the squash into 1/2-inch circles. Keep the skin on.
3. Cut the eggplant lengthwise into 1/2-inch thin strips.
4. Grease a baking dish lightly or line with parchment paper. Place squash and eggplant in the dish and bake for 10 minutes. Turn over and bake for additional 10 minutes.
5. Take out of the oven and top with cheese and veggies. Return to oven for another 20 minutes or until veggies are done.
6. Serve immediately or freeze for later.

VARIATION: Another choice of crust would be sweet potato or zucchini.

• If you wish, you can make Butternut Squash Pizza Bagels. Use the thick end of the squash, remove the seeds, and follow the rest of the recipe. This is a fun activity for children.

Thai Chili Basil Fried Rice

by Benjamas Musignisarkorn (Thailand) (gluten-free)

Ira and Benjamas Musignisarkorn, the owners of Swadee: House of Thai Food, were born and raised in Thailand. Swadee: House of Thai Food was established by their aunt Sunee Indranak in 1994. Ira and Benjamas gained cooking experience by helping their aunt run the restaurant when they had time off from school. They have continued their aunt's vision of making the best Thai food with the healthiest and freshest ingredients after their aunt retired. Visit Swadee: House of Thai Food at 886 Franklin Ave., Thornwood, New York.

Serves 2-4

1 medium-size red bell pepper

4 garlic cloves

3 bunches cilantro root

2 tablespoons vegetable oil

3 tablespoons soy sauce

1/2 teaspoon black pepper

10 slices white onion

1 cup mixed vegetables of your choice, sliced

2 cups jasmine rice, cooked and preferably chilled

3 branches scallions, chopped

15 basil leaves

spicy fresh chili or chill flakes (optional)

salt and sugar (optional)

DIRECTIONS:

1. In a blender, process bell pepper with garlic and cilantro root.

2. In a pan, heat the vegetable oil. Add the bell pepper mixture, soy sauce, black pepper, white onion, and mixed vegetables. Stir-fry until vegetables are almost cooked.

3. Add cooked jasmine rice and continue stir-frying until the rice is hot.

4. Add the scallions and basil leaves. Do a taste-test for flavor. Add chili, salt, or sugar until it reaches your desired taste.

VARIATIONS: Add tofu.

• If you can't find cilantro root, use one bunch of cilantro leaves.

Escarole and Bean Will Make You Lean

by Dolly Winters (Italy) (gluten-free)

Dolly Winters is the mother of Bill Winters and my mother-in-law. She is third generation of Italian descent living in Westchester, New York. She enjoys gardening, preparing family dinners, and attending Zumba classes. In her family, food is love. She prepares fresh and healthy food for her family as her mother and grandmothers have done. Bill and I love this dish! *Mangia!*

Serves 6-8

2 large heads fresh escarole

8-10 large cloves garlic

1/4 cup olive oil

2 (19-ounce) cans white cannellini beans

salt and pepper to taste

lemon juice, for serving (optional)

nutritional yeast, for serving (optional)

DIRECTIONS:

1. In a large pot of water, place escarole and bring to a boil. Reduce heat. Cook until tender and drain.

2. Sauté garlic in olive oil until translucent. Do not let garlic brown.

3. Stir in small amounts of escarole at a time. Simmer for 10 minutes.

4. Add beans with liquid from can and stir carefully. Simmer for 10 minutes.

5. Serve with lemon juice and nutritional yeast if you wish.

MUJADARA
by Tava Naiyin (gluten-free)

Tava is a professional belly dancer and author in the NY/tri-state area. Tava dances for communities from the near East to North Africa and the Gulf. Spending so much time in Moroccan, Lebanese, Persian, Greek, and Turkish restaurants and participating in cultural events has really opened her palate. This particular dish is Lebanese, but she has added a few variations. Food is such a wonderful doorway to various cultures and has the power to transport people back home when they eat the dishes from their countries of origin. Food, just like dance, unites us. It is a bridge for which she is eternally grateful.
www.BellydancebyTava.com

Serves 2
1 cup brown or green lentils
1/2 cup olive oil
1 teaspoon cumin seeds or powder
1/2 teaspoon black peppercorns or pepper
3–5 onions, thinly sliced
1 1/2 teaspoons plus a pinch salt
1 teaspoon cumin powder
pinch cayenne powder, if you like it spicy
cinnamon stick
3/4 cup basmati rice
vegan yogurt

DIRECTIONS:
1. In a medium saucepan, add lentils and enough cold water to cover them by about an inch. Bring to a boil over medium-high heat. Turn down to a simmer and cook for about 20 minutes. Drain and set aside.
2. While the lentils are cooking, heat a large skillet over medium-high heat and add oil. Drop in the cumin seeds and cracked peppercorns and cook for about 1 minute.
3. Add onions and a pinch of salt and cook until onions turn dark caramel brown. This will take about 15 minutes. Remove about half of the onions for garnish for later.
4. Sprinkle in the ground cumin and cayenne, and then add the cinnamon stick. Sauté for about 1 minute.
5. Add rice and cook until some rice grains start to brown, stirring often. Add the cooked lentils, 3 cups water, and the remaining 1 1/2 teaspoons salt. Bring to a boil. Turn the heat down to low so that the pan is at a simmer. Cover and cook for 30 minutes.
6. Turn off the heat, keep the lid on, and allow the rice to steam undisturbed for about 5 minutes.
7. Serve with the reserved caramelized onions and a spoonful of plain almond or coconut yogurt.

NORWEGIAN VEGGIE STEW
by Hilda Brevig (Norway) (gluten-free)

Hilda Brevig is a life artist. Her favorite quote is, "Be the change you wish to see in the world." She loves animals and nature. She speaks six languages and has five degrees. She runs a real estate company and works as a photographer. She studied photography in Bali, Italy, and Norway. She wants to make the world a better place by eating clean, organic food; respecting the planet and all living beings; and promoting health and happiness. She resides in Norway.
www.fotografhilde.no | www.veganfood.no

Serves 4
3 carrots
2 potatoes
1 yellow onion
1 red onion
1 parsnip
1/2 head cauliflower
1/2 bunch broccoli
1/4 rutabaga
2 tablespoons vegetable stock
water and coconut milk, enough to cover the vegetables
1 tablespoon turmeric
salt
pepper

DIRECTIONS:
1. Chop all vegetables.
2. Place vegetables in a pot and pour in water and coconut milk until they're just covered. Add the stock and spices.
3. Boil for 10–15 minutes. Turn the heat off and leave the cover on. Wait for about 20 minutes.
4. Serve with some crisp bread or flatbread. It pairs well with **Olenko's Mom's Bread (see recipe page 98).**

CAULIFLOWER GARDEN PIZZA MAMMA MIA
by April Carter (Inspired by healthy California Cuisine) (gluten-free)

April Carter is a freelance movie trailer editor and lives in Malibu, California, with her husband, Sean, and new baby, Gabriel. She enjoys yoga, spinning, and hiking. As a busy mom trying to encourage a healthy lifestyle for herself and her family, she is always on the lookout for recipes that are nutritious, easy, and most importantly, delicious.

Serves 2-4
Crust:
3 tablespoons flax seeds plus 3 tablespoons warm water
1 medium head cauliflower
1/4 cup coconut flour
2 tablespoons almond flour
1/2–1 tablespoon chopped fresh rosemary
1/2 teaspoon garlic powder
1/4 teaspoon salt
Toppings:
Not Your Mom's Mozzarella (see recipe page 87)
Garden Pizza Mamma Mia Sauce (recipe follows)
fresh basil
pineapple
red onion
red chili flakes

DIRECTIONS
1. Make the crust: Combine flax seeds with water and set aside.
2. Use a box grater or food processor to grate the cauliflower. Transfer to a double boiler and steam over medium heat until soft.
3. Place cooked cauliflower in a fine mesh sieve and squeeze out excess water. (I use a nut milk bag, but you can use any method you like as long as you can get as much water out as possible.)
4. Preheat oven to 400°F.
5. Place the cauliflower in a bowl and add remaining crust ingredients. Mix well by hand until all the ingredients are well incorporated and the mixture resembles dough. Form it into a ball, and then flatten and form into a flat disc, 8–10 inches in diameter.

6. Bake crust for about 25–30 minutes, or until it starts to turn golden brown.
Add toppings:
7. Remove crust from oven. Lower the oven temperature to 350°F.
8. Spread mozzarella on crust first to help seal the cracks in the crust. Then spread on the pizza sauce. Add pineapple and red onion as desired. Sprinkle with chili flakes.
9. Slide pizza back in the oven and cook for additional 10 minutes, until cheese is melted and the crust starts to color on the edge.
10. Remove from the oven and let cool for a minute or two. Sprinkle with fresh basil and a dash of red chili flakes for added spice.

GARDEN PIZZA MAMMA MIA SAUCE
by April Carter (gluten-free)

1 onion
2 cloves garlic
1/2 teaspoon salt
1/2 teaspoon black pepper
1 (12-ounce) can tomato sauce
1 tablespoon oregano
1 teaspoon garlic powder
pinch crushed red pepper
pinch ground cinnamon

DIRECTIONS
1. Place onion, garlic, and remaining seasoning in a small saucepan. Cook over medium heat for 2–3 minutes or until fragrant and onions become translucent.
2. Add remaining ingredients and bring to a boil. Lower the heat and simmer partly covered for 15–20 minutes, until sauce is thickened and all water has evaporated.
3. Serve with **Cauliflower Garden Pizza Mamma Mia.**

CHAPTER 15

Nature's Gifts from the Bar

Occasionally, we feel like having a drink to celebrate a birthday party or a holiday. Unfortunately, many of those drinks are very unhealthy and contain lots of sugar and artificial colorings. Here are fun, inspired-by-nature alternative versions of alcoholic drinks that my husband and I created for home entertaining. Remember to always drink responsibly. For every alcoholic drink you consume, make sure you drink a glass of water to stay hydrated. For fun-effect ice cubes, place edible flowers, small fruits–such as berries–and small pieces of herbs into ice cube trays. Cover with water or coconut water and freeze. Enjoy in your drinks or water.

CANTALOUPE WINE SLUSHY

Serves 6–8
1/2 ripe cantaloupe, peeled and cubed, plus extra pieces for garnish
1/2 bottle red wine

DIRECTIONS:
1. Freeze cantaloupe cubes.
2. Place wine and frozen cantaloupe in a high-speed blender and blend until smooth. You can add ice if you want.
3. Serve in a glass with a piece of fresh cantaloupe on the side. Enjoy on a hot day or as a cocktail.

VARIATION: Blend fresh cantaloupe with wine and pour into popsicle molds to create a refreshing snack for adults for a pool party or BBQ.

KEEP IT CLEAN PIÑA COLADA

Serves 2-4
5–6 ounces rum
1/2 cup coconut milk
2 Medjool dates, pitted
2 cups cubed pineapple, frozen
2 ripe bananas, frozen

DIRECTIONS: Mix all ingredients in a high-speed blender. Add crushed ice if desired. Serve topped with a slice of pineapple and fresh or frozen cherries. Add more coconut milk if you prefer thinner texture.

Puerto Rican Chia Coquito

by Regina Ramirez (Inspired by Puerto Rican Cuisine)

Regina Ramirez is an elementary public school teacher in Yonkers, New York. Although not a vegetarian or vegan, she loves to include bountiful amounts of fresh fruits and vegetable dishes in her diet. She enjoys gardening and growing her own fruits, herbs, and veggies, and spending time with family and friends. She believes that healthy food not only makes your taste buds happy, but it also awakens the possibilities of a happier and healthier lifestyle. When making this cocktail, you can add more rum to taste. I did! Refrigerate for at least an hour. It is best served very cold, but you can always include pretty ice cube shapes or ice chips. Garnish with shredded coconut and cinnamon.

Serves 8-10

1/2 tablespoon chia seeds

3 tablespoons water

1 (13.6-ounce) can unsweetened coconut milk

1 (13.6-ounce) can coconut cream

2 tablespoons maple syrup

7-10 large Medjool dates (depending on how sweet you want it), pitted

2 teaspoons vanilla extract

1/2 teaspoon cinnamon

1/2 teaspoon nutmeg

1/2 teaspoon allspice

1/2 teaspoon ground cloves

1/2 cup white rum (I use Bacardi)

DIRECTIONS:

1. Soak chia seeds in water.
2. Place the remaining ingredients except rum in a blender.
3. Add chia seeds (the chia seeds add thicker consistency and creamy texture).
4. Add rum and blend well. Enjoy!

VARIATIONS:

• If you like your Coquito really spicy, use 1 teaspoon of each spice powder.
• If Coquito is too thick, add 1 cup coconut water or coconut milk (not from a can).
• For a holiday treat, add 1 cup pumpkin puree and/or a ripe persimmon.
• Pour mixture into popsicle molds and freeze to create refreshing treats for adults.

SIMPLY THE BEST WATERMELON VODKA COOLER

Serves 6

3 pounds watermelon
3 tablespoons lime juice
3 tablespoons lemon juice
1/2 cup vodka
fresh mint

DIRECTIONS:

1. Place the watermelon in a high-speed blender and blend. Strain through a mesh strainer or a nut milk bag and use the juice to make the drink (you may discard the pulp).
2. Add lime and lemon juice and mix well.
3. Serve over ice. Garnish with fresh mint, a slice of watermelon, strawberries, or a slice of cucumber.

SEARCHING FOR THE SUNRISE SANGRIA

Serves 6–8

1 (750-milliliter) bottle dry red wine
2–3 ripe peaches, sliced
1 1/2 cups strawberries, sliced
2 purple plums, cubed
1 sweet apple
1 large orange, cut crosswise
1 large lemon, cut crosswise
1–2 tablespoons maple syrup (optional)
fresh mint

DIRECTIONS: Cut all the fruits and combine in a large pitcher with the wine and maple syrup, smashing citrus slightly. Let sit at room temperature for 2–4 hours. Serve over ice with fresh mint.

DREAMING OF THAI BLUE MALIBU

Serves 4

2 cups Thai Pea Flower tea, room temperature
2 frozen bananas
1 cup coconut milk
2 tablespoons coconut butter
3 Medjool dates, pitted
2 ounces rum
lemon wedge

DIRECTIONS:

1. Prepare the tea to create blue color and strain the flowers.
2. Place bananas, coconut milk, coconut butter, dates, and rum in a high-speed blender and mix until smooth.
3. Transfer tea and blended mixture to a tall glass. Squeeze the lemon juice right before serving and watch how the color changes from blue to purple.

THE DAY THE SUN DANCED MOJITO

Serves 1

2 1/2 ounces rum
juice of 1/2 lime
juice of 1/2 lemon
2 tablespoons coconut sugar
1 cup ice
10 fresh mint leaves
fresh cane sugar, for garnish

DIRECTIONS:

1. Using a shaker, mix rum with lime and lemon juice. Add sugar, ice, and mint leaves.
2. Serve in a tall glass with cane sugar.

SIMPLY THE BEST IRISH COFFEE WITH COCONUT WHIPPED CREAM

Serves 1

3/4 cup hot coffee
1–2 tablespoons coconut sugar
1 1/2 ounces whiskey
Coconut Whipped Cream

DIRECTIONS:

1. Using a shaker, combine all ingredients and shake well.
2. Serve in a glass topped with a spoonful of **Coconut Whipped Cream (see recipe page 151).**

VARIATION: For a frozen variety, use cold coffee with the rest of the ingredients. Add 1–2 scoops of raw banana ice cream and drizzle some warm raw chocolate over the top.

OPEN YOUR HEART POLISH MULLED WINE

Serves 6–8

Mulled wine:
1 (750-milliliter) bottle red wine
1 orange, sliced
1 lemon
1/4 cup maple syrup or coconut sugar
6–7 whole cloves
3 star anises
1/2 teaspoon cinnamon powder
1/4 teaspoon cardamom powder
1/4 teaspoon nutmeg powder
Garnish:
3–4 cinnamon sticks, for garnish
3–4 oranges, for garnish

DIRECTIONS:

1. Make the mulled wine: Combine the wine with the spices and fruits in a large saucepan and simmer over low heat for about 10 minutes.
2. Garnish: Pour into mugs and serve with cinnamon sticks and orange slices.

I'm Not Gonna Lie, I Like Some Tonic with Thyme
by Bill Winters

Bill Winters is my husband. He is an award-winning director of photography specializing in TV commercials, documentaries, music videos, and branded content. Bill's work has appeared in numerous publications, including the prestigious American Cinematographer Magazine, International Cinematographers Guild Magazine, The New York Times, The Wall Street Journal, Variety, and Entertainment Weekly. In addition to motion picture work, Bill is an accomplished photographer with many cover shoots and celebrity portraits, including Barack Obama, Bill Clinton, LeBron James, Jerry Seinfeld, Lenny Kravitz, Mike Tyson, Tom Cruise, and Halle Berry. Bill photographed my beautiful food for this book—and then ate it!
www.billwinters.net

Serves 1

2 ounces Bourbon
2 ounces seltzer water
1 cup ice
juice of 1/2 lemon
1 tablespoon maple syrup
1 sprig fresh thyme, for garnish
lemon slice, for garnish

DIRECTIONS:

1. Using a shaker, combine all ingredients and mix well.
2. Serve in a glass with sprig of fresh thyme and a slice of lemon.

CHAPTER 16

I Was Born That Way: Simply the Best Natural Beauty Care!

Have you ever wondered how come you are so cute? You were born that way! Are you in love with yourself? Are you grateful for your body? Do you take the time to pamper yourself and get a massage or a facial? Do you ever spend a whole day in your pajamas, sipping tea, and watching movies? Life is too short, so take the time to take care of yourself. If you don't have time to go to a spa, create your own home-spa. Find your own truth and allow yourself to be supported. You are love. You deserve to have a glorious life and a beautiful body.

In this chapter, you will find many simple recipes for your health, beauty regimen, and self-care. Did you know that you can create natural, organic, chemical-free beauty products in your own kitchen? Your skin is the largest organ in your body, so use only natural, organic skin-care products without harmful ingredients. Let your imagination go wild and make your own beauty care products with your family and friends.

Feel confident in your own skin. Take good care of your skin, hair, and body. Start making your own beauty and skin-care products with natural ingredients, such as essential oils, coconut oil, olive oil, argan oil, aloe vera, and avocado. Remember to get plenty of fresh air and sun. Stay hydrated, exercise, and follow a healthy rainbow diet. Namaste.

EXFOLIATING FLAXSEED FACE MASK FOR RADIANT GLOW

2–3 tablespoons golden or brown flax seeds
1–2 tablespoons rose water
1 teaspoon clay powder
1/2 teaspoon turmeric powder (optional)

DIRECTIONS:
1. Soak flax seeds in 1/2 glass of pure water for 5–12 hours or overnight.
2. Add remaining ingredients. Mix well. If the mixture is too thick, add a few drops of water. (If you want to get a really good exfoliating experience, use whole flax seeds. If you want a gentler exfoliation, blend the flax seeds in a high-speed blender, and then add the rest of the ingredients.)
3. Apply the mask to your skin. Make round moves over your face, avoiding eyes.
4. Leave mask on for 15–20 minutes. Wash it off with warm water, and follow up with a **Natural Citrus Face Toner (see recipe page 192)** and **I Feel and Look Fabulous Body and Face Cream** (see recipe page 192).

SCRUMPTIOUS BODY SCRUB

1 tablespoon sea salt
1/2 cup extra virgin olive oil (you can substitute sweet almond oil or Moroccan argan oil)
1 teaspoon organic lemon zest
4–5 drops of your favorite citrus essential oil, such as grapefruit, lemon, lime, or lemongrass
1 cup dark brown sugar

DIRECTIONS:
1. In a mixing bowl, combine all ingredients except brown sugar and mix.
2. Add brown sugar and mix well.
3. Use immediately or store in a glass jar and use later in the shower or bathtub. This scrub is great to use before shaving your legs. (Please be aware that oil in the scrub can make the shower and bath surfaces very slippery.)

RAW CACAO SUPER ANTIOXIDANT FACE MASK

(basic recipe)
1 tablespoon raw cacao powder
2 tablespoons clay powder (you can use Moroccan clay)
1/4 teaspoon maca root powder
1/2 teaspoon turmeric powder
1/2 teaspoon jojoba oil, olive oil, almond oil, or argan oil
1 cup steeped and cooled organic green tea
1–2 drops therapeutic grade essential oil, such as lavender or Frankincense

DIRECTIONS:
1. In a small bowl, mix together dry ingredients. Add oil.
2. Add cooled green tea, one spoon at a time, until mixture reaches a creamy, pudding-like consistency. Add essential oils if you wish.
3. Apply a thick layer over face and neck. You can put sliced cucumbers on your eyes and relax for 10–15 minutes. Wash it off with warm water. Follow with **Natural Citrus Face Toner (see recipe page 192)** and **I Feel and Look Fabulous Body and Face Cream** (see recipe page 192).

COOLING BODY SPRAY FOR HOT SUMMER DAYS

1 cup water
3–4 drops peppermint essential oil, therapeutic grade
2–3 drops lavender essential oil, therapeutic grade

DIRECTIONS: In a spray bottle, mix all ingredients well. Spray on the legs or back of the neck to feel refreshed during hot summer days. Store away from the sunlight.

ESSENTIAL OIL HAPPY LIQUID SOAP

1/4 part castile soap
3/4 parts water
5 drops peppermint essential oil
5 drops lemon essential oil
5 drops eucalyptus essential oil

DIRECTIONS: Mix all ingredients in a glass dispenser. Experiment with different essential oils, such as lime, geranium, lavender, tea tree, orange, lemongrass, Frankincense, and rosemary.

CHAPTER 17

Live Your Life With Joy and Eat Your Food with Joy, Because the Rainbow Diet Is the Best Diet!

Eat the

Radiant
Alignment
Intuition
Nature
Beauty
Olenko's Kitchen
Whole-foods

Diet

If you feel stressed out, sick, and out of alignment, your body and mind must be brought to balance in a holistic and synergetic way. You must ground yourself. Planet Earth, our Mother, has a natural healing pulse. We are part of nature, so going back to it is the simplest way to get aligned and centered.

When you locate your own heart center and follow your own inner truth, you will find balance. By going outside and walking barefoot on the grass, sand, or snow, you connect yourself with the electromagnetic pole of Planet Earth. By being in nature and feeling the natural elements of the wind, sun, fresh air, trees, water, grass, birds, flowers, and fruits, you infuse your body, mind, and

soul with nature's gifts. By grounding yourself with the earth through your feet, you activate the root chakra. You can also eat grounding natural foods, such as root vegetables: beets, carrots, turnips, potatoes, onions, celeriac, etc.

We are supported by the earth. Computers and technology are very helpful, but we must remember to live our lives in balance. By creating a simple visualization and imagining yourself surrounded by blue, purple, and golden light coming from the sun, moon, and stars, you activate your solar plexus and crown chakra.

Diffuse essential oils—such as Frankincense, lavender, lemongrass, orange, and balsam fir—to activate the healing process. Use fruits, vegetables, herbs, and spices to help you cleanse and detox your body. Surround yourself with crystals that have healing properties. You can also burn dry sage or Palo Santo. This practice has been used by many cultures around the world and is great for cleansing your energy.

Singing bowls, belly dancing, African dance, singing, chanting, praying, yoga, meditation, healing baths, flower mandalas, and listening to the wind, rain, or birds chirping can be very helpful in assisting you with healing and connecting with nature. Drinking lots of water, herbal teas, and fresh coconut water is very beneficial and can help you find your alignment. Getting connected with your inner self by balancing your inner rainbow/chakras will help you find healing energy within. Sleeping on a BioMat is soothing to your muscles and will help you ground yourself.

Your inner world is a reflection of your outside world. When we let go of judgment, self-criticism, memories, negative beliefs, victim mentality, and physical and mental pain, we become free. Natural food and nature will easily assist us with this process. When we surround ourselves with positive thoughts, positive people, and healthy food—and when we perform simple practices, such as walking in the woods or on the beach—we find inner peace and connection with the cosmos, God, and our own soul. We, as a species, have a huge responsibility to help

SPIRITUALITY AND FOOD

Our body is our biggest source of information. You are with your body twenty-four hours a day for your entire life, so listen to the messages it tries to communicate to you. Find your inner truth by asking questions about what is right for you regarding food and outlook on life. Be careful what you consume daily: I am referring to food and your emotions.

If you feed your body with unhealthy processed foods, live a stressful life, are unhappy about your job or relationships, complain about everything, and are surrounded by miserable people who pull you down, you may become out of alignment and even sick. Be careful who you spend time with, and watch out for food addictions and cravings. Be mindful of your body's responses. If something doesn't agree with you, simply let it go.
Very often we get stuck and are unable to let go

"When you arise in the morning, give thanks for the morning light, for you life, and strength. Give thanks for your food and the joy of living. If you see no reason for giving thanks, the fault lies in yourself."

– Tecumseh

ourselves, other earthlings, and our children. There are so many children with food sensitivities, so we must teach them about the clean and natural rainbow diet. When we are negative, fearful, stressed out, and focused on lack, we become detached from inner self and attract diseases. When we choose love instead of fear; when we believe that the world is full of abundance, beauty, colors, and love; and when we share natural foods with others, then we find love, compassion, and joy. By taking care of our body, mind, and soul, we can assist and help others. By being generous with kindness, we spread positive messages of love and joy.

Find what natural practices work for you and use them in your everyday life. Check with yourself several times a day to see how you feel. When you feel out of alignment again, go for a short walk, meditate, drink a glass of water, breathe deeply, etc. These simple practices will help you stay in a heart-centered place.

of things, people, memories, habits, or food that doesn't serve us anymore. Food is energy, and emotions are energy. Ask questions and see how you react to them.

Setting an intention for your life is crucial. When you wake up every day, set an intention for the day. Concentrate on joy, happiness, well-being, prosperity, creativity, fun, and fulfilling experiences with family, friends, and coworkers. This positive energy will carry you throughout the day and help you inspire others as well.

Sometimes the truth is right in front of our eyes, but we can't see it. The truth will set you free! You are your own best teacher. Be brave and look inside your soul. All your answers are inside of you. Remember that transformation is a process that may happen instantaneously or take a very long time, so be gentle with yourself. Be your own best friend and treat yourself with kindness, love, and compassion. Be patient with your feelings.

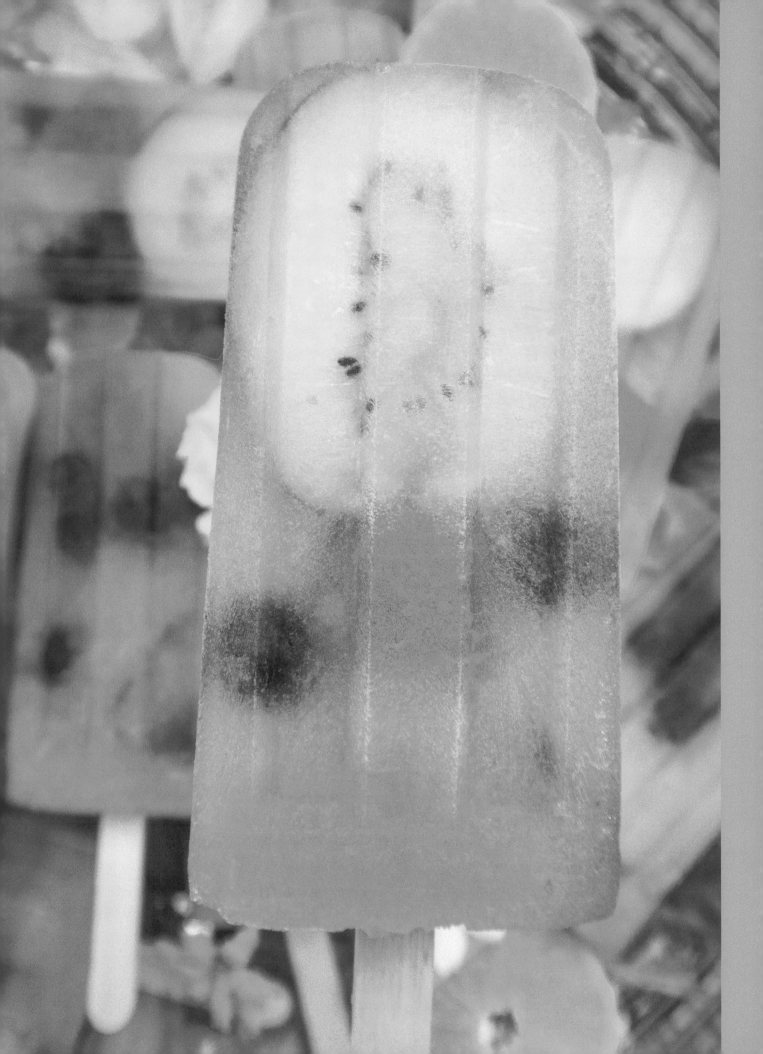

Of course, sometimes it is very helpful to work with a specialist—such as a doctor, coach, acupuncturist, or herbalist—to help you with your transformation, but your positive mind-set will have the most significant impact on your healing, recovery, and spiritual journey. The path is yours; listen to your heart and find your own answers. Find joy in simple everyday moments. Relax and don't be too serious about your life. Look into the stars and find beauty in nature. Remember that life is supposed to be easy and joyous. You are loved! The universe loves you and wants you to succeed in your journey. All is well. *Namaste.*

YOUR RELATIONSHIP WITH FOOD

I cook with love and savor the time when I make my meals. I eat slowly to enjoy the rainbow of flavors. I have a healthy relationship with food. If your relationship is not so good, understand that attitude and emotions toward the food you consume play a much more important role than you think. If what you eat makes you feel guilty afterward, change the

way you feel about food. Negative emotions about what you eat may attract sickness, diseases, and weight gain.

Make food your friend, not your enemy. Don't obsess with counting calories, and don't deprive yourself by starving. Enjoy your food and eat the rainbow. Eat food that comes in its natural state. Make choices based on what is in season. If you do that, your body will thank you.

The way you feel while preparing your food is equally important. Think positive and loving thoughts. You don't want to consume food that has been charged with negative energy. Make your food with love and joy, and in turn it will bring love and joy to your body.

A happy, fulfilled person may enjoy comfort food and not experience any side effects. However, if you are not happy or satisfied with your life in general, eating healthy may not be enough. In such case, practice an attitude of gratitude and joy, and learn how to look at life from a broader perspective of love and appreciation.

Food Cravings

Pay attention to what's going on when you have a craving. How do you feel at the moment? Are you under stress? Sad? What emotion triggered the craving? Cravings usually have an emotional basis or nutritional deficiency.

Remember that we all have a special relationship with food. On a physiological level, we need

"Just as food is needed for the body, love is needed for the soul."

– Osho

food to sustain us. However, many times we give in to food cravings and use food for emotional gratification, such as when we are bored, upset, unhappy, frustrated, or depressed. Don't hate your food cravings. Your body is trying to communicate with you. Listen to your cravings and treat them as messages from your body.

Sometimes we crave something because it brings memories of a time that we cherish from our past or childhood. It may be an emotional response to a situation. It may remind us of traditional food in our culture, or there may be a biological or hormonal cause. Opt for healthier substitutes for your cravings. For example, choose dates, sweet fruit, or raw cacao treats instead of candy. Nuts, seeds, seaweed, kale chips, celery juice, pickles, sauerkraut, nut cheese, and fruit dipped in nut butter make healthier options for salty snacks.

Don't use processed sugar or processed flour. Make healthy, flourless bread. You can still eat your favorite comfort food, but modify the recipe to make it healthier. Use whole ingredients, such as fruit and vegetables, instead of processed ingredients. Make a habit of offering something healthy to your children instead of processed snacks. Don't buy unhealthy snacks so you won't be tempted to eat them.

When you have a craving, consider the following:

- You may be dehydrated and only think you're hungry. Drink plenty of water throughout the day. If you don't like plain water, infuse it with fruit, such as lemon or lime; herbs, such as mint or basil; or cucumbers.
- If you crave chocolate, you may be deficient in iron, potassium, and magnesium. If you crave salty snacks, you may lack iodine.
- If you crave cheesy and greasy food, you may lack hot flavors and spices in your diet. Try adding cayenne pepper, ginger, turmeric, hot jalapeño pepper, or cinnamon to your food.
- Many times people snack on unhealthy food when they watch television or feel bored. Choose juicy fruit instead of candy, and guacamole or hummus with cut-up veggies instead of popcorn. Have a smoothie instead of soda, and a fruit or banana popsicle instead of heavy ice cream. Surround yourself with healthy food to always have healthy options available.
- If you have been following the standard American diet and eating empty calories, your body may be craving nutrients. You would not have drastic cravings if you were on a whole plant-based diet.
- You may be sleep-deprived, and your body may be trying to compensate by tricking you into cravings for things like coffee or pizza. Take a nap, go to bed early, and have herbal tea, green juice, or a smoothie. Use essential oils.
- Do something nice for yourself, like have a massage or go for a walk. Do something fun, such as go dancing, watch a comedy, or sing karaoke.
- Ask yourself how often and at what time of the day you usually have a craving for something sweet: first thing in the morning, after lunch, after dinner, before bedtime, or as a snack between meals? Talk with a doctor or naturopath to see if you need a blood test to detect if you are deficient in any minerals and vitamins.
- Keep a journal of the foods you eat throughout the day to help you discern patterns that may not serve your health.
- Write a loving letter to your body to apologize for having abused it with food that doesn't serve you at the moment and to forgive yourself.
- Some cravings may be seasonal. In the winter, you may crave comforting, warm food. Choose hearty food, such as root vegetables, and warming spices,

such as cardamom, nutmeg, and cinnamon. Eat more soups and stews. In the summertime, cool your body by choosing cucumbers, watermelons, salads, smoothies, and juices. Don't forget to drink lots of water or coconut water.

- Some food cravings may be a sign of a health condition, such as low blood sugar, low blood pressure, pre-diabetes, or diabetes. Consult a health professional to find out if your food cravings have any biological cause.
- Fluctuation in hormone levels during menstruation, pregnancy, or menopause may cause food cravings. Consult a medical professional to discuss these cravings.
- If you occasionally give in and splurge on something unhealthy, kiss self-sabotage goodbye and let a health coach help you discover healthy options for your diet

Having a Goal

There are many specialists who will tell you to set a goal before you start a diet or another health regimen. While having a goal is certainly important, do not forget that the ultimate goal for all mankind is to be happy and enjoy life. If one of your goals is to lose weight, do not obsess about the perfect weight you want to achieve, and do not deprive yourself of food that could be beneficial to you.

Craving the foods that you forbade yourself from eating could sabotage your goal. When you focus on what is not allowed or what you perceive as bad, you unintentionally obstruct the process and don't reach the goal. Maybe you measure each portion and meticulously count calories, and then feel guilty if you exceeded your benchmark. Maybe you had one too many pieces of chocolate than you think you should have.

The lifestyle that I promote—a lifestyle, not a diet—is based on an intuitive and natural approach: listen to your body and nature, eat pure food, and don't count calories. Nobody has ever said, "I ate too many cucumbers, and I'm gaining weight!" No matter what you do, do not obsess about the end result. Just enjoy the process. The more open you are to joy and receiving good things, the sooner these will manifest in your life.

More Tips for Healthy Living

- Drink juice and a smoothie every day
- Eat a huge salad for lunch
- Substitute whole food for junk food
- Eat local organic food whenever possible
- Cook at home
- Drink water
- Reduce drinking of soda and sugary drinks
- Avoid fast food restaurants
- Eat more fruits and fewer unhealthy desserts or snacks
- Be grateful for everything in your life
- Stay positive
- Forgive
- Indulge in self-care
- See beauty in everything around you
- See goodness in people
- Have compassion
- Live your life with joy
- Help someone
- Take up a hobby
- Spend time in nature
- Play with a pet
- Use essential oils
- Pay a compliment
- Get plenty of sleep and rest
- Take naps throughout the day to recharge
- Go earthing (walk barefoot to connect to the Earth)
- Love
- Exercise
- Rest
- Smile
- Laugh
- Breathe
- Meditate
- Practice Yoga
- Dance (notice that the word 'abundance' comprises 'dance')
- Imagine yourself happy all the time
- Eat the rainbow diet every day!

When striving to reach your goal, be sure to do the following:

- Concentrate on what you can do, as the mind doesn't really respond to can't.
- Decide what your priorities are regarding healthy living, and vote for them with your dollar. Choose to buy organic and non-GMO products, support local farming, visit farmers' markets, and buy from people who care about the environment, animals, and renewable resources instead of from big corporations.
- Buy whole-food ingredients instead of premade packaged food. Most food that comes premade contains some kind of preservatives, even the "healthy" products, because they need to last on the shelf and still look fresh. Whole foods, on the other hand, spoil easily because they are free of preservatives. For example, when you cut an apple, it will turn brown because of a natural chemical reaction called oxidation.
- Grow your own fruits, vegetables, and herbs. In the summer, you can grow them outside, and in the winter, bring the pots with herbs inside. If you live in an apartment and do not have a garden, experiment with microgreens kits or grow kits for indoors. You can also experiment with sprouting seeds and nuts.
- Include many raw fruits and vegetables in your diet. Raw food is extremely beneficial, as it contains healing properties and vital enzymes.
- Infuse your food with love and positive energy as you are making it. Put in a good intention and enjoy the process of making your meals, as everything is vibration and energy.
Bless your food before you eat it.

Be happy

Be joyful

Sparkle more

Shine your beautiful light

Live your life with passion

Peace begins with you

Namaste

CHAPTER 18

I'm Not Going to Deny that I Like to Shop for Nature's Goodies Online

Here are some of Olenko's favorite websites and places to buy specialty ingredients.

Rainbow Food:

www.therawfoodworld.com

www.sunfood.com

www.nuts.com

www.frontiercoop.com

www.mikesorganicdelivery.com

www.miamifruit.org

www.bragg.com

www.thepathoftea.com

www.americantearoom.com

www.medicineflower.com

www.e3live.com

www.markusrothkranz.com

www.7hotdates.com

www.healthytraditions.com

www.us.foursigmatic.com

www.rawnice.com

www.bluechai.com

www.teeccino.com

www.veganessentials.com

www.amazon.com

www.healthytraditions.com/tropicaltraditions

www.thrivemarket.com

www.coconutsecret.com

www.livingnutritionals.com

www.shamanshackherbs.com

Essential Oils:

www.youngliving.org/billwinters

Grocery Stores:

Whole Foods

Trader Joe's

HMart

Mrs. Green's

Spiritual Jewelry:

www.indigorevolve.guru

www.spiritualboho.com

www.facebook.com/essentialoilpendants/

Spirituality:

www.akashiclighthealing.com

www.marinajacobi.com

www.denaearias.com

Healthy Living:

www.OlenkosKitchen.com

www.medicalmedium.com

www.nyack-acupuncture.com

www.nailspaelmsford.com

www.ariahairandbeauty.com

www.fmlifestyleinc.com

Cruelty Free Fashion:

www.thewomaneveryday.com

www.kasiaethicalware.com

Vegan Restaurants:

www.vitaparadise.com

www.riverdelcheese.com

www.dunwelldoughnuts.com

www.cinnamonsnail.com

www.chickpeaandolive.com

www.candle79.com

www.jolosrestaurant.net

www.blossomnyc.com

www.beyondsushinyc.com

www.peacefoodcafe.com

eatbychloe.com/sweets/

www.thebutchersdaughter.com

For The Love of Animals:

www.peta.org

www.mercyforanimals.org

www.aspca.org

www.farmusa.org

www.farmsanctuary.org

www.veganoutreach.org

www.cok.net

www.friendsofanimals.org

www.vegansociety.com

www.woodstocksanctuary.org

www.casanctuary.org

www.panacealv.com

Retreats:

www.facebook.com/Sanctuary-of-Peace-and-Healing-1869922126589967/